An overview of all the crucial
passages on women's roles

WOMAN
—in the Bible—

Mary J. Evans

Foreword by Donald Guthrie

InterVarsity Press
Downers Grove
Illinois 60515

Published in the United States of America by InterVarsity Press, Downers Grove, Illinois, with permission from The Paternoster Press, Limited, England.

InterVarsity Press is the book-publishing division of Inter-Varsity Christian Fellowship, a student movement active on campus at hundreds of universities, colleges and schools of nursing. For information about local and regional activities, write IVCF, 233 Langdon St., Madison, WI 53703.

Distributed in Canada through InterVarsity Press, 860 Denison St., Unit 3, Markham, Ontario L3R 4H1, Canada.

Unless otherwise stated, the Scripture quotations in this publication are from the Revised Standard Version of the Bible, copyrighted 1946, 1952, © 1971, 1973 by the Division of Christian Education of the National Council of the Churches of Christ in the U.S.A., and used by permission.

Cover illustration: Roberta Polfus

ISBN 0-87784-978-1

Printed in the United States of America

Library of Congress Cataloging in Publication Data

Evans, Mary J.
    Woman in the Bible.

    Bibliography: p.
    1. Woman–Biblical teaching.   I.   Title.
BS680.W7E83   1984   261.8'344   84-4641
ISBN 0-87784-978-1

17	16	15	14	13	12	11	10	9	8	7	6	5	4	3	2	1
97	96	95	94	93	92	91	90	89	88	87	86	85	84			

To
Jo and Sylvia

Foreword ——— 7

Introduction ——— 9

I. Old Testament ——— **11**

1. Old Testament: Doctrine ——— 11

   a. The Creation Narratives ——— 11

   Genesis 1 ——— 12

   Genesis 2 ——— 14

   Genesis 3 ——— 17

   b. Elsewhere in the Old Testament ——— 21

   Imagery Used to Describe God ——— 21

   Freedom from Oppression ——— 22

   Corporate Personality ——— 23

   The Song of Solomon ——— 23

2. Old Testament: Practice ——— 24

   Woman in Society and the Family ——— 24

   Woman in the Worship of the Covenant Community ——— 26

   Woman in Office ——— 29

3. Old Testament: Conclusion ——— 31

II. Contemporary Cultural and Religious Influences ——— **33**

1. Judaism ——— 33

2. Essenes and the Qumran Sect ——— 37

3. The Graeco-Roman World ——— 38

4. Contemporary Influences: Conclusion ——— 41

III. The Gospels ——— **44**

1. Gospels: Introduction ——— 44

2. Jesus' Approach to Women ——— 45

   Women as Subjects Not Objects ——— 45

Women in Everyday Life —— 47
Women Used in Parables —— 48
Women as Responsible People —— 48
Women as Followers and Disciples —— 49
Women in Theological Conversation —— 51
3. Women in the Passion Narratives —— 53
4. The Attitude of the Disciples —— 55
5. The Gospels: Conclusion —— 56
6. Excursus: Mary the Mother of Jesus —— 57

IV. Acts and Epistles: Doctrinal Teaching —— 61
1. Paul: Woman in Relation to God —— 62
2. Paul: Woman in Relation to Man (I) —— 64
Introduction —— 64
Headship, Authority and Submission —— 65
3. Paul: Woman in Relation to Her Husband —— 69
1 Corinthians 7 —— 69
Ephesians 5:21-33 —— 73
Colossians 3:18-19 —— 77
1 Thessalonians 4:3-6 —— 78
1 Timothy 5:14 —— 78
Titus 2:1-6 —— 79
Woman in Relation to Her Husband: Conclusion —— 80
4. Paul: Woman in Relation to the Church Community —— 81
Worship —— 81
1 Corinthians 11:2-16 —— 82
1 Corinthians 14:34-36 —— 95
1 Timothy 2:8-15 —— 100
Woman in Worship: Conclusion —— 107
Leadership —— 108
5. Paul: Woman in Relation to Man (II) —— 113
6. Paul: The Relation of Christian Women to Those outside the Christian Community —— 115
7. Other New Testament Doctrinal Teaching —— 116
Hebrews 13:4 —— 116
1 Peter 3:1-7 —— 116

V. Acts and Epistles: Community Practice —— 122
1. Marriage —— 122

2. Official Ministries _____ 123
    Apostles _____ 124
    Elders and Bishops _____ 124
    Deacons _____ 125
    Teachers _____ 126
3. In the General Life of the Churches _____ 126
    The Church at Jerusalem _____ 126
    The Church at Rome _____ 127
    The Church at Philippi _____ 128
    In the Other Churches _____ 129
    Community Practice: Conclusion _____ 129

VI. Conclusion _____ **131**
Bibliography _____ 134
Notes _____ 142

ABBREVIATIONS

Bib.Arch.	Biblical Archeologist
BJRL	Bulletin of the John Rylands Library
Calv.Th.J.	Calvin Theological Journal
CBQ	Catholic Biblical Quarterly
Ch.	The Churchman
Ch.Tod.	Christianity Today
DNTT	*New International Dictionary of New Testament Theology* (C. Brown, ed., Paternoster, Exeter, 1975–78)
Ecum.Rev.	Ecumenical Review
Eg.et Th.	Eglise et Théologie
Exp.T.	Expository Times
Hist.Rel.	History of Religions
ICC	International Critical Commentary
JAAR	Journal of the American Academy of Religion
JBL	Journal of Biblical Literature
JCBRF	Journal of the Christian Brethren Research Fellowship
JETS	Journal of the Evangelical Theological Society
J of R	Journal of Religion
JTS	Journal of Theological Studies
NCB	New Century Bible
NLC	New London Commentary
NTS	New Testament Studies
Rev.Bib.	Revue Biblique
SJT	Scottish Journal of Theology
St.Ev.	Studia Evangelica
TDNT	*Theological Dictionary of the New Testament*, (G. Kittel ed., Eerdmans, Grand Rapids, 1964)
Th.St.	Theological Studies
W.Th.J.	Westminster Theological Journal

The tractates of the Talmud are abbreviated as in H. Danby *The Mishnah* O.U.P., London 1933.

FOREWORD

There is no doubt about the importance of the subject of this book. The modern debate about the role of women in the church has been approached from many points of view, and especially relevant is the question of the ministry of women. Although there are several treatments of the subject which appeal to the biblical evidence, not many of them concentrate on an exegetical approach.

There are inevitably problems in dealing with a subject of this kind, particularly in a male-dominated society. When books are written by men about women's role, many women fear that a male bias has dictated the approach. Similarly when women write about their own role, even more men are likely to regard the effort as another advocacy of the feminist cause. Although the present book is written by a woman, it is hoped that the latter prejudice will not prevent a careful examination of the exegetical evidence.

Mary Evans is well qualified to undertake this task. She is a careful scholar who approaches the text with a genuine desire to discover its meaning. She is certainly not a militant feminist. Not all will agree with her exegetical conclusions, but they will discover that she marshalls her evidence in a fair manner and carefully weighs up the issues involved. It is valuable to have this treatment of the subject which is written from a feminine point of view but which is nevertheless thoroughly based on the biblical text.

I am glad of the opportunity to write this foreword, not only because the major part of this book formed a thesis prepared under my supervision, but more especially because of my personal regard for the author as a friend and colleague.

Donald Guthrie

INTRODUCTION

There has been much discussion in recent years on the place of women in the church, much of this discussion being centred round the question of which activities or functions, within the community of the church, women should or should not be permitted to take part in or carry out. The question has been approached from various angles. Many have appeared to follow the approach of Freud, who in discussing the 'problem' of femininity says, 'Nor will you have escaped worrying over this problem – those of you who are men; to those of you who are women this will not apply – you are yourselves the problem.'[1] Others have acknowledged more explicitly that the church itself is made up of both males and females. Some of these see sexuality as the major factor in the organizing of the church community so that what one actually does within the church is primarily influenced by whether one is male or female. Others have assumed that while each person has a part to play within the Body of Christ specifically as male and female, the primary contribution of each is as a Christian, with sexuality playing only a minor part in the living out of their lives as Christians.

In general, for the Christian who accepts the inspiration and authority of the Word of God and who is concerned that life should be lived according to biblical principles, there are two distinct areas of investigation. Firstly, we need to discover precisely what the Bible does have to say on the subject and secondly to decide just how this should affect our attitude and behaviour today. The importance of this second area, the application of biblical teaching in today's world, is fully recognized, but in this study we will be concentrating almost entirely on the first area. What does the Bible actually say about the place and role of women and about the relationship between men and women?

It is often assumed that any biblical teaching on this matter will be culturally conditioned and therefore irrelevant or at least able to be safely ignored. Others take it for granted that we know what the Bible says and our only problem is to make certain that its teaching is applied in the churches; any change in attitude or even any consideration of the area must therefore be inspired by cultural considerations from our own time and be in opposition to biblical teaching.

Neither of these approaches is correct. It is arbitrary to dismiss any biblical teaching as culturally conditioned without a strong indication within the context that cultural influences have been a primary consideration, and this indication is very rarely present. We must take Scripture seriously, taking fully into account both doctrinal teaching and the way that teaching was applied. However, it is inevitable that our own thinking has been conditioned by philosophical and cultural presuppositions[2] in a way that has strongly influenced our interpretation of Scripture, and, as we shall see, has sometimes even directly affected translation. In a changing world then, it is vitally important that we re-examine the biblical material, not to alter it, not to ignore it and not to fit it in with the ideas of modern society, but to make sure that we have got it right and that our ideas and practices really are biblical and not just reflecting the philosophical presuppositions of a by-gone age, or indeed of our contemporary society.

What we are attempting to do in this study is to investigate what the Bible has to say about women and their role. In particular we are concerned to discover how the New Testament church as a whole regarded its female half, how big a part the fact of their being female played in the lives of the women within the Christian community, and how far any differences between male and female roles and functions were related to theological presuppositions and principles.

In order to do this we have looked firstly at the doctrinal teaching of the Old Testament and the practical application within the Old Testament community and then considered the background influences on the developing New Testament church, influences which come not only from the Old Testament, but also from the cultural and religious conditions in the contemporary world. In the New Testament, we have looked firstly at the way in which Jesus and the Gospel writers approached women. We have then considered the doctrinal teaching given in the epistles regarding the place of women in the New Testament church community with regard to the family, to the worship and leadership of the church and to society outside the church. Finally we have looked at the practical life of the individual church communities.

A number of books and articles on the subject have been produced in the interval between the completion of the script and its publication. Some of the most relevant of these have been included in the bibliography even though they are not specifically referred to in the text.

1

Old Testament

1. OLD TESTAMENT : DOCTRINE

Any study of the theological aspects of the relationship between men and women in the Old Testament must start with the account of the beginning of that relationship in the Creation narratives. In fact, outside these early chapters of Genesis there is very little specific doctrinal teaching relating to this matter, although certain themes, such as the imagery used in describing God, are relevant and must therefore be considered.

It will become clear that in a society where religious and national life are almost synonymous, the connection between doctrine and practice is a very close one, and we can learn much from the practice of the people about their understanding of doctrinal principles. However, there are contained within the Old Testament many theological insights which the nation, as their prophets repeatedly told them, failed to appreciate or to apply correctly. Thus doctrine and practice are not synonymous and it is therefore valid to consider doctrinal points separately from those which arise from a study of daily living, though the link between doctrine and practice and the necessity of using the one to interpret the other must always be kept in mind.

a. The Creation Narratives

The two separate accounts found in chapters 1 and 2 of Genesis approach creation, and in particular the creation of male and female, in a different manner. They stress different points and answer different questions. Genesis 1 presents a worked out theology of the creation of the universe with the creation of Man* as the apex of the account. Genesis 2 also contains theology, but within the context of the narrative; the account concentrates on a garden planted by God in one particular corner of the universe, and has the creation of Man as the focal point. Both accounts have much to teach us and the differing insights provided can and should be brought together, but because of the differences between them we must always be wary of assuming that questions raised in one account can automatically be answered by arguments drawn from the other.

Genesis 1

Genesis 1:26 immediately makes a distinction between Man and the rest of the created beings. Man was created as the result of a particular decision on the part of the Creator – 'Let us make Man' – created with a special relationship to God – 'in our image, after our likeness' – and given a specific task to do – 'Let them have dominion'. Verse 27 sums up the situation: 'So God created Man in his own image, in the image of God he created him; male and female he created them.'

Thus the Genesis 1 account tells us that the distinction between the sexes is there from the very beginning, inherent in the idea of Man; the creation of mankind as male and female is an integral part of God's decision to make Man. Two complementary conclusions can be drawn from this; firstly that 'the idea of Man... finds its full meaning not in the male alone, but in man and woman,'[1] and secondly that the human personality must be expressed in either male or female form. 'There is no such thing as a human being apart from a man or a woman.'[2]

Sexual distinction in creation therefore is quite clear. Nevertheless in this account there is no distinction between male and female in their creation as in the image of God or as in having dominion over all the earth. No hint of subordination of one sex to the other can be found here. The blessing and commission of verse 28 in no way excludes or limits the female part of Man. 'Mankind is immediately created as two sexes and is as such entrusted with the free lordship over the rest of creation.'[3] It is only in relatively recent times that an interest in ecology has caused questions to be raised as to the meaning and perhaps the limits set on Man's

* In order to avoid confusion, when it is used in a generic sense, relating to mankind as a whole, Man is printed with a capital letter.

lordship over creation. These questions are important but have no direct relevance to the fact that whatever the nature of the responsibility Man does have for creation, Genesis 1 places that responsibility on the shoulders of both men and women.

In contrast, there has been a great deal of debate about what it means to say that Man is created in the image of God, and about the content and nature of that image.

P. K. Jewett[4] identifies three theological options for understanding Man as the image of God. Firstly, when the image is seen in mankind as a whole, so that the totality of Man is needed in order to express the image of God. In this case, the male-female dichotomy has no real significance. Secondly, when the image of God is seen in each individual whether male or female. This is the traditional view, although there have been those among the Church fathers who have argued that the image of God can be seen only in males and not in females.[5] Thirdly, there is the view put forward by Barth, which Jewett himself holds, that the image of God can be seen only in male and female together, that it exists between them rather than as part of either. Brunner's view of Man reflecting the image of God in every relation, not just the sexual relation, seems to fit best here, although Jewett sees it as a development of the traditional view.

It is true that Genesis 1:27 does seem to show a connection between Man as in the image of God and Man as male and female, and that the traditional view completely neglects this point. Aquinas does not mention the male-female relation in any of the nine articles in which he deals with the divine image.[6] It may be that Barth's idea of the image of God as an 'analogia relationis' rather than an 'analogia entis', that is, as something that can be seen in 'relationship' rather than in 'being' as such, may have some light to shed, particularly when we keep in mind his stress on the fact that any understanding of what the image of God means can be in the nature of an analogy only.[7] However, Genesis 5:1–3 does imply that the image can be and is passed on, and passed on to an individual, and Genesis 9:6 also supports this position as well as indicating that the image of God in Man is not lost by the Fall. (These two references can incidentally be used to support the rejection by Christian theology generally of the first of Jewett's three alternatives.) It must always remain to some extent a mystery, and perhaps there are both individual and relational aspects of the way in which Man reflects the image of God. What is clear is that 'Genesis 1 gives us no reason to think that woman participated in the image of God in any way different than man.'[8]

If there is little information in the Old Testament as to exactly how the image of God is to be seen, there are many who have sought to describe what it implies within Man. Some would see it in a concrete sense implying some sort of physical similarity, others more in terms of religious or ethical qualities.[9] There are certain ideas which suggest that women possess the characteristics of which the image consists, or in which it results, in a different way from men and only these are relevant for our purposes.

Genesis 1:26 and to some extent Psalm 8 show a connection between the divine image and likeness in Man, and his dominion over the rest of creation. Many writers take this up and assuming that the aspect of dominion is stronger for men than for women conclude with Calvin that the woman was created in the image of God, 'though in the second degree'.[10] The arguments used to support this secondary image in women are drawn not from Genesis 1, where there is no indication of any difference, but from Genesis 2. As Genesis 2 does not discuss the question of the divine image, the validity of arguments drawn from there is not self-evident. Nevertheless, we must investigate whether or not there is anything in Genesis 2 to suggest that women reflect the image of God in a different or lesser way than men.

Genesis 2

There are four main arguments used to show that Genesis 2 teaches the subordination of the woman to the man, and thus his dominion over her, as a 'creation ordinance'.

    a. Woman was created after the man and is therefore secondary to him.
    b. Woman is 'taken from the man' and is therefore secondary to him.
    c. Woman is named by the man and is therefore subordinate to him.
    d. Woman is created to be a 'helper' for man and as such is subordinate to him.

When the cumulative effect of these arguments is considered, they appear to be conclusive, but their cumulative effect is of course dependent on their individual validity which we must now consider.

    a. Does temporal priority of creation in itself imply superiority of either being or function? In Genesis, to assume that being created first implies superiority in any sense must mean that chapter 1 implies that the animals are superior to Man and chapter 2 that they are superior to women. The text clearly suggests neither of these things, therefore the force of the argument is lost. In fact, there is no indication in Genesis 2 itself that temporal priority is of any particular significance. The chapter appears to fit well into the ring construction of Hebrew thought, where the central concerns of a unit appear at the beginning and end.[11] The two creatures, male and female, are thus seen as parallel, the order disparaging neither one. It is true that Paul in 1 Tim. 2:13 refers to the fact that Adam was created before Eve; although Paul himself does not draw out the implications of this. Calvin makes an interesting comment here: 'The reason which Paul assigns, that woman was second in the order of creation, appears not to be a very strong argument in favour of her subjection.'[12] However, if subordination is not to be found in the Genesis creation narratives when interpreted within their historical context, then it is possible that Paul also is not using the argument in that way; but we will return to 1 Timothy 2 at a later stage.[13]

b. The argument that woman being 'taken from the man' implies her being secondary is more telling. E. Jacob is convinced by it that Genesis 2 teaches the subordination of women: 'Man by himself is a complete being, the woman who is given to him adds nothing to his nature, whilst the woman drawn forth from man owes all her existence to him.'[14] However, apart from the fact that the chapter could be seen as indicating that without the woman the man is himself incomplete, the whole emphasis of the later verses of Genesis 2 is not on the difference between male and female but on their relatedness. Adam recognizes and responds to Eve firstly as someone like himself, identified with himself, rather than as different from or other than himself. The point of emphasising that the whole of mankind came from one ancestor is that it establishes both the absolute unity of humanity, and the identical substance of both male and female[15], in a way that could never be true if there had been separate creations from dust.[16]

Woman is created from the rib of the man, but it is important to note that it was the direct creative act of God in building up the rib that gave the woman her being, not the rib itself. She is 'taken from the man', but, 'Her first and primal contact is with her Maker. Woman herself knew God before she knew her counterpart, the man.'[17] As Trible puts it, 'Man has no part in making woman ... he is neither participant nor spectator, nor consultant at her birth. Like man, woman owes her life solely to God. For both of them, the origin of life is a divine mystery.'[18] Thus we see that even derivation is not a strong argument for subordination. It is wrong to say that woman owes all her existence to man, just as it would be wrong to say that man owes all his existence to dust and is therefore subordinate to it. Both man and woman are portrayed as created directly by an individual and purposeful act of the Creator.

c. The third argument is that naming in the Old Testament times implied dominion and that the man in naming the woman (Genesis 2:23) is thereby exercising dominion over her. However, given that on some, though by no means all, of the occasions of naming within the Old Testament an exercise of authority of the namer over the named is involved, one should note that in the standard naming formula we find both the verb 'to call' and the noun 'name'; as for example in Genesis 4:25 'she bore a son and called his name Seth.'[19] It will be noted that in Genesis 2 these words are found together only in verse 19, when the animals are brought to Adam to be named. In verse 23 the noun 'name' does not occur. Similarly it must be noted that the word 'woman' is never used as a proper name, it is simply a common noun designating gender. Thus verse 23 can be seen as something other than an official naming and thus again the strength of the argument is lessened. Genesis 3:20 where after the Fall Adam 'called his wife's name Eve' does contain the formula and must be considered later.

d. The fourth and most widely used argument is that woman is made as man's 'helper' and as such is automatically subordinate to him. This argument convinces both Knight, who writes, 'It is simply the proper application of concepts and realities to affirm that if one human being is created to be the helper for another human being, the one who receives such a help has a certain authority over the one who is his helper',[20] and Vriezen, who sees woman as 'the helpmate of man, his complement and partner ... fundamentally his equal, but secondary, although man, as a social being cannot do without her.'[21] The 'common sense' approach is not particularly strong either way, though one wonders whether Knight's argument would convince doctors whose raison d'être is to be of help to their patients that they are in some way under the authority of those patients. However, it remains necessary to investigate whether a 'helper' as described in Scripture is necessarily subordinate or secondary. Vos shows us that of the nineteen times the word is used in the Old Testament, one is in a question, in three it is used of man,[22] where incidentally in each case the help is not effectual, and in fifteen it is used of God bringing succour to his needy people.[23] The word 'helper' could therefore conceivably be interpreted as suggesting superiority, though in this case the accompanying 'fit for him' (i.e. 'worthy of him', or 'matching him') removes this possibility. It can be said, however, that the use of the word 'helper' of itself cannot be seen as implying inferiority or subordination in any sense. The helper fit for man is his counterpart, his complement, his partner, his companion and his associate, bone of his bone, and flesh of his flesh. There is no evidence at all to support Augustine's theory that the woman was to be a helper only in childbearing but that in every other case another man would be a better help.[24] In fact this view might be said to be directly contradicting the teaching of Genesis 2.

Thus we are left with Jewett's conclusion: 'So far as Genesis 2 is concerned, sexual hierarchy must be read into the text, it is not required by the text.'[25] There is no need for us to see Genesis 1 and Genesis 2 as antithetical, one teaching the equality of the sexes in creation and one the subordination of one sex to the other. Certainly there is nothing in Genesis 2 which would lead us to assume that woman has the image of God in a different or lesser way than man. Both chapters show that Man as a whole consists of two parts, the man and the woman. Each is seen as a complete individual, but what is stressed here is not their individuality or the difference between them, but rather their unity and the fact that they are 'indissolubly bound together'.[26] The Creation narratives could certainly never be used to support the extremist 'Women's Lib' thesis that woman can exist in total independence of man.[27] They rather teach that human life in every sphere can be fully lived only as male and female cooperate together.

One cannot separate the relation between man and woman here from the relation between man and wife, although it is not until Genesis 2:24 that marriage as such is mentioned. Marriage is the example 'par excellence' of the complementarity and partnership of the sexes. It is interesting to note that far from supporting patriarchalism, Genesis 2:24 sees the man, rather than the woman, leaving home to 'cleave' to his wife. The verb 'cleave' here is used almost universally for a weaker cleaving to a stronger. It is used of Israel, cleaving to God (e.g. Joshua 23:8; Psalm 91:14), but never the other way round. It is perhaps significant that this verse should have survived in an androcentric culture like Israel's, though the verse is in no way meant to propose the dominion of either sex but rather the total communion between man and woman in a marriage relationship, and the priority of that relationship even over that between a man or woman and their parents.

Genesis 3

In Genesis 3 we have a very clear picture of the way in which the relationship between the man and the woman was spoiled by sin. We are not concerned here with the full significance of the Fall or with all its implications for mankind but simply with what we can learn from the chapter about the relationship between man and woman and the effect that the Fall had on that relationship. We will consider first of all the sin itself, as described in verses 1–6, and then the consequences of and the punishment for the sin which are dealt with in the rest of the chapter.

The serpent tempted the woman, seeking to persuade her that the result of disobeying God was something to be desired – good for food, a delight to the eyes, and to be desired to make one wise. John's warning against the lust of the flesh, and the lust of the eyes and the pride of life (1 John 2:16) stands as a salutary reminder that the temptations to which the woman yielded were not left behind in the garden. The woman did yield. She took the forbidden fruit, ate of it, gave it to the man and he too ate. The total communion between the man and the woman described in Genesis 2:24 is thus emphasised before it is broken. The woman's first and natural reaction is to share with the man the fruit that she has taken. The man does not need to be led, he merely assents. Westermann calls this the negative side of their oneness relation, pointing out that 'social laziness can only occur in community'.[28]

There have been many suggestions as to why the woman, rather than the man, was approached by the serpent,[29] but these can be conjecture only as the narrative maintains total silence on the point. However, although we have no way of ascertaining whether or not the man was present throughout the episode or only at the end, Genesis 3:7 makes it clear that it was only when both had taken the fruit and eaten that 'the eyes of *both* were opened and *they* knew that they were naked.' They sinned and fell as individuals but also as a pair. It is important to note that the sin involved here is disobedience. As the chapter goes on to tell us, one result of that sin was the disruption of their relationship, but there is nothing whatsoever in the text that would lead us to assume that part of the woman's sin was in usurping the position that should have belonged to the man. There is no indication that in acting as she did she 'sought to control' the man.[30] The woman is presented as acting as an independent being, as making a decision herself before she turned to the man, but there is no hint anywhere in the chapter that she was condemned for this. Paul tells us (2 Cor. 11:3; 1 Tim. 2:14) that Eve was deceived, but she appears to have been deceived as to the results of her action rather than as to its rightness. Her sin, like that of the man, was simply disobedience.

That the man and the woman were punished for their sin shows that God was taking them both seriously. They had been created as responsible beings and were therefore treated as such. But of what did their punishment consist? It is a common assumption that Genesis 3:16 describes the punishment of the woman, the curse of God on her, with Genesis 3:17–19 similarly being the curse of God on the man. In fact, as a closer reading makes apparent, it is only the serpent, in verse 14, and the ground, in verse 17, that are described as cursed; neither the woman nor the man is described as under God's curse. Westermann is perhaps right to see the punishment of the couple as consisting of their expulsion from the garden which ensured their removal from the sphere of the tree of life and the consequent death of which God had warned. If this is so, then verses 14–19 'merely develop what it means for man to be driven out of the presence of God. They are not really punishments, they simply describe the actual state of man separated from God.'[31] That is, they describe the inevitable consequences of Man's sin, whereas in verses 22–24 we find the actual punishment described.

Sin inevitably led to the disruption of the relationship between Man and God (cf verse 8). This in turn led to the disruption of the relationship between man and woman and between Man and the ground. However, to see either of these disruptions as the permanent will of God for Man and to treat their results as abiding law is surely to misunderstand the purpose of the text. It must always be recognized that Man's sin has effects which go far beyond the sinner, as for example the effect on the families of imprisoned criminals. These effects are inevitable, but it cannot be assumed that it is wrong to seek to offset them. Thus man weeds his garden and seeks to ease his burden of toil with technology. Similarly medicine is used to ease pain in childbirth, and there appears to be no reason why the disruption of relationship described in the second half of verse 16 should not similarly be eased.

Traditionally the latter half of verse 16, 'Your desire shall be for your husband and he shall rule over you', has been interpreted as implying that because the woman desires the husband he is able to rule over her. This 'desire' is variously interpreted as referring to sexual desire, to 'the desire that makes her the willing slave of man',[32] as including the desire for protection[33], or as such that she will desire only what her husband desires.[34] However it could be said that none of these interpretations is adequate, in that if a woman is a willing slave or without desires of her own, the rule of the husband will have none of the hardship that is implied by the context. Etymology of the word 'desire', *tesûcah*, is difficult as it occurs only three times in the Old Testament;[35] but S. Foh[36] is of the opinion that it is more likely to have its origin in the Arabic root *sāqa*, to urge, to drive on, than in *šāqa*, to desire. She then sees desire in Genesis 3:16 in the sense of desire to rule, and in doing so takes into account the close parallel in structure and vocabulary of Genesis 4:7 where Cain is tempted to sin.

If desire has the same meaning in both these verses then Genesis 3:16 can be interpreted as indicating that the woman will have a desire to possess or control her husband, but in fact, he will rule over her. The hardship is that the sexual relation which should have been one of co-operation and complementarity has become primarily one of conflict and competition. It should be pointed out that 'the words of the Lord in Genesis 3:16, as in the case of the battle between sin and Cain, do not determine the victor of the conflict.'[37] However, they may be seen as predictive; in the social system as it was, and indeed as it has generally been throughout the centuries, the man would be predominant.

To interpret desire in this way, fits with the context, recognizes the parallel between Genesis 3:16 and Genesis 4:7 and explains the fact that husbands do not always rule their wives nor wives desire their husbands in the way that any of the more traditional interpretations would imply. In the conflict situation arising from the disruption, due to sin, of the relationship between the sexes, the woman will, in general, be dominated. However, in spite of his being dominant the man also suffers in this conflict situation, as the woman suffers in the conflict with the earth, although this is presented as primarily affecting the man. Genesis 3 does indicate that the effects of sin come upon men and women differently but does not really uphold Luther's opinion that 'the female sex... bears a far severer and harsher punishment than the men.'[38]

Thus the narrative of Genesis 3 with its description of the events and consequences of the Fall provides an explanation, although not necessarily a justification, for the male domination in the Israelite society. It shows that a profound change took place in the relationship between men and women as a result of sin. Where there had been communion there would now be conflict; where there had been equality there would now be domination. D. S. Bailey views the antagonism between the sexes as a result of 'that immemorial androcentricity which has corrupted...relationships'.[39] However, it seems more likely that the androcentricity is itself the result of the previous disruption of relationships caused by the Fall.

Of course it has always been possible, even in pagan societies, for Man to offset some of the worst consequences of the Fall, if only temporarily, and it must be remembered that the close relation between the sexes, though spoiled, still exists. Nevertheless, however much the results are offset, the conflict situation remains.

It is only 'in Christ' that the broken relation between man and woman, as that between God and Man, can fully and permanently be restored. It is outside the scope of this study to ask what such a full and permanent restoration could and should mean, but it is a question that all Christians should be asking at some stage.

An application of the results of the Fall is seen straight away in Genesis 3:20 where the man, this time using the standard naming formula, 'called his wife's name Eve', demonstrating his authority over her. It is interesting to note that Eve is still honoured here as 'the mother of all living'; an attitude to women not found elsewhere in the Ancient Near East.[40] Perhaps this is an indication that although woman was seen as secondary in the Israelite society she was nevertheless honoured in her own place and misogyny as such was not usual.

Genesis 1–2 presents man and woman as different but united, each the perfect complement of the other, each playing his or her part in the God-given tasks of filling and governing the earth (Genesis 1:26–28). Genesis 3 shows us the disruption of this relationship. It is not the relation as such that is destroyed, but rather its perfection. Man and woman are still complementary but no longer perfectly so. Life outside of Eden must be lived with all the conflicts and tensions that were the inevitable result of Man's disobedience to God.

b. Elsewhere in the Old Testament

Imagery Used to Describe God

If God is male, then the relation of the human female to God will naturally be different from that of the human male. In a society where religious and social life were so closely linked, this in itself would provide justification for the androcentricity of the society and would be the cause of the subordinate and secondary role of the female. In fact in later Judaism, the maleness of God was used to legitimate male dominance.[41]

However, in spite of the strong preponderance of the masculine gender in metaphors and other imagery describing God, 'there is a strong consensus that the Old Testament regards Yahweh as non-sexual'.[42] It can be said that the character of God as revealed in the Old Testament 'implicitly disavows sexism'.[43] Both anthropomorphisms and andromorphisms are repudiated where they could be seen as limiting God. That is, though there is a very free use made of imagery it is always made clear that the imagery is to be recognized as such. Deuteronomy 4:16 tells us that since God is not seen, it is quite wrong to assume that any image 'in the likeness of male or female' can be made, and certainly wrong to attempt to make such an image. God is complete, whole and therefore above sexuality; he is not to be pictured as either male or female.

It is possible that the use of masculine terminology is more a reflection of 'the status of male and female in society . . . than an indication of the status of male and female respectively before God'.[44] Paul Hanson sees the dominance of male metaphors as a product of a society with 'patriarchal structures predicated upon sexual inequality' and therefore feels that the use of these metaphors for reinforcing such structure is inadmissible.[45] In a patriarchal society, the characteristics which are assigned to God are generally those which males assign to themselves as ideal. Therefore in such a society it is significant that feminine imagery, though not common, does occur. It is interesting to note that, although in the Church all language about God is masculine, in Scripture this is not so.[46]

God is seen as providing food[47], water[48], and clothing[49] for his people, all of which are acknowledged as women's work. Martin Noth,[50] commenting on Numbers 11:12 where Moses asserts that he is not the mother of the people, says, 'Implicit in this is the very unusual idea that Yahweh himself is Israel's Mother', and sees the verse as 'indirectly attributing to Yahweh the concept of femininity'. More explicit feminine terminology is used elsewhere[51] with God being described as midwife, seamstress, housekeeper, nurse and mother. The fact that such feminine imagery is found at all in relation to God, means that we cannot really use the preponderance of the masculine imagery as an argument for differentiating between male and female in their relation to God, nor can we use it to support hierarchy in their relation to each other.

Two further points must be noted in connection with this. Firstly, imagery, whether masculine or feminine, remains imagery. It can help us relate to God, it can give us great insight into the character of God, but it cannot define or delimit God. Secondly, to describe God as non-sexual is not in any way to assume that he is non-personal, although to us sexuality and personality are so closely linked and perhaps even inseparable.

Freedom from Oppression

The principle of freedom from oppression is inherent in the Old Testament. The foundation of Israelite history is the Exodus, where Yahweh released his people from slavery. Yahweh is presented as having a special concern for the underdog, for the poor, for the widows and orphans.[52] The Messiah would come to proclaim liberty.[53] The Old Testament itself presents freedom from oppression for women as meaning that they should be treated kindly and well within whatever is seen as their proper sphere, rather than that they should be freed from that sphere. It should be noted that any secondary status of women does not necessarily imply oppression, but if that secondary status is seen as a result of the Fall rather than as a natural created state – as for example in the case of the animals – then it could also be termed oppression. Maybe then, the 'latent potentiality for liberation'[54] found in the Old Testament can legitimately be used as a tool to help restore the male-female relation spoiled by the Fall; but the Old Testament itself makes use of such a principle only to offset the worse effects of that broken relation.

Corporate Personality

The Old Testament concept of corporate personality can be seen as relevant to this issue in two ways. Firstly, in the solidarity of the family where, 'in terms of personal identity there is not a clear distinction made between a man, his possessions, his wife and his animals'.[55] This leads to the concept of the man worshipping on behalf of the whole family and also explains the references where the wife appears to be linked with possessions.[56] It was not so much that the wife was seen as a possession, but rather that, in one sense, the possessions were, like the wife, part of the man himself.[57]

Secondly, the concept of national solidarity means that in so far as one part of the nation was oppressed or enslaved the whole nation suffers.[58] Thus, if any oppression of the women of Israel did exist, it was damaging not only to the women themselves, but also to the nation as a whole.

The Song of Solomon

Trible interprets the Song of Solomon as a midrash on Genesis 2–3, showing a return to the relation between the sexes lost by the Fall.[59] Whether or not this is so, it is evident that in the Song of Solomon the 'mutuality of the sexes' is clearly affirmed . There is no male dominance, no female subordination, and no stereotyping of either sex. The woman is independent, fully the equal of the man. Her interests, work, and words defy the connotations of "the second sex".' It is apparent that the Song of Solomon does not in any way present us with a picture of normal Israelite life. The book is limited also in that it does not relate Man to God and in that it makes no reference to sin and disobedience. But it does show that in Old Testament thought the concept of mutuality and equality between the sexes could be envisaged as possible and even perhaps as desirable, although again it must be stressed that the concept is rarely found worked out in practice within the Israelite society.

2. OLD TESTAMENT : PRACTICE

Woman in Society and the Family

It was usual for women to be considered, not in their own right, but in relation to the man under whose authority they were placed. As Ryder Smith explains, the Old Testament conception of their status in society is determined almost completely by the valuation which was placed upon them by their husbands and sons.[60] The fact that the father was the legal head of the household and that every woman was always under the authority of some man, first her father and then her husband,[61] is perhaps the key to the way in which the Israelite women were treated.

Smith is of the opinion that women were really viewed as chattels but occasionally did come to be seen as persons in their own right. Mace, on the other hand, thinks that they really were viewed as persons, but just occasionally were debased to the level of chattels.[62] He sees two major factors influencing this; firstly, that the blurring of distinctions between wives, who had certain legal rights and 'could appeal to their own families for redress', bondwomen, who had very few rights, and concubines, who were more than slaves, but less than wives, led to a lowering of the status of women in general. The wife might find herself treated as a slave and vice-versa.[63] Secondly, Mace sees no clear distinction between the authority of the husband or father, and ownership by him, which again leads to confusion in attitudes. The woman, in relation to her sexuality was owned by her husband, which is why the adultery and divorce laws are in the category of property laws, but her person remains her own. 'As far as her sex goes she is her husband's property; but in her person she is not possessed by him and may in fact rank as his equal, or even (as in the case of Abigail –

1 Samuel 25) his superior.'[64]

Given the subordinate status of the wife, her actual position in the family and the way she was treated varied. As Vos points out, there are no rules for delineating the subordination of the wives, nowhere is the wife told to honour or obey her husband, there are no regulations for dealing with the disobedient wife, as there are for children.[65] The patriarchal structure of society and in particular the family was not justified by a doctrinal theory, nor by the law, but rather it was simply taken for granted, based 'on the certainty that the soul of the man is the stronger.'[66] In the Hebrew concept of honour the stronger always comes before the weaker, which explains their apparent lack of chivalry![67] The normal leader of the family was undoubtedly the male. 'Round the man the house groups itself, forming a psychic community which is stamped by him. Wives, children, slaves, property are entirely merged in this unity.'[68] However, in certain cases the soul of the man was not the stronger, and if so, then 'it may happen that the patriarchate cannot be absolute, for every man has in him the kindred of the mother as well as the father.'[69] Certainly, though the patriarchal structure was very strong, female leadership within a family was not unknown. The Shunamite woman in 2 Kings 4 was by no means averse to taking the lead in her family structure, nor was Abigail, or even Sarah (Genesis 21:12).

At times, the wife is seen merely as a means of obtaining children,[70] for to every Israelite to have children, especially boys who would carry on his line, was vitally important. However, there are many indications that a wife was seen also as a person in her own right and valued as such. Proverbs 31 certainly presents the wife as much more than a bearer of, and nursemaid for, a man's children; in fact, in this ideal picture of a wife, children are mentioned only incidentally. Rather, 'as her husband's trusted partner she has sole responsibility in her domain which extends beyond the house to the management of her lands and to dealings in the market.'[71] It must be noted that this picture does describe an ideal rather than an actual situation, but it is interesting to observe how much this ideal picture differs from the generally accepted stereotype of Old Testament womanhood.

As far as the legal position of women is concerned, many have agreed with Mendelsohn that 'a recital of the position of the Hebrew woman according to the law paints a gloomy picture of her legal and economic status.'[72] It is certainly true that in the literature of the Ancient Near East there are laws which favour women more than those of Israel. For example, the Code of Hammurabi allows women to inherit along with their brothers and if they are divorced, makes material provision for them.[73] J. L. McKenzie points out that women in Israel, like children and slaves, could not make moral decisions;[74] their oaths, for example, had to be ratified by husband or father before they could become valid, for the women did not have the freedom which moral responsibility of this kind entails.

The picture may, as Mendelsohn suggests, be gloomy, but it is not all black. Vriezen quotes the conclusion of Reifenberg that the existence of the names of women on Hebrew seals shows that women were in fact 'persons from a judicial point of view'.[75] Women were bound to keep all the moral precepts of the law, and this was their own responsibility, not that of father or husband. The Israelite women did have rights, both legal and economic, but these rights 'were secured and safeguarded for them, not by themselves, but by the men under whose authority they were at the time'.[76] Maybe Eichrodt is right to note that where family ties are strong, legislation is often unnecessary.[77] It perhaps explains also why those who have no family to safeguard their rights, such as widows with young children, are seen as being under the special protection of Yahweh.

Thus we have a picture of the Israelite women, subordinate to their husbands and generally of lower status than men. They were seen for the most part as child-bearers, or at best homemakers, but in some cases they were acknowledged as companions and partners, and it was not impossible for them to have wider spheres of interest and work. How they were treated and the sort of life a woman lived depended largely on the attitude of her husband and on his position in society.

Woman in the Worship of the Covenant Community

There was a preponderance of male participation in the worship of Israel, as the man, being the leader of the household, played the major part in most cultic acts. This, together with the fact that only males underwent circumcision, which was the sign of the covenant, has led to conclusions like those of Koehler[78], who in describing the scope of the covenant says, 'It is a covenant with those who are competent to enter into such a thing; that is to say with the men; they represent the people . . . woman has no place in this revelation, therefore she is a constant danger to the worship of Yahweh.' However, Eichrodt,[79] 'The congregation of Yahweh includes the family, . . . neither age nor sex bestow any special privileges' and Jewett[80], 'In ancient Israel women shared with men in the grace of

God as members of the covenant community ' – come to a different conclusion.

The covenant relationship between God and his people involved blessings and responsibilities. We must inquire how far the women of Israel received the blessings and how far they shared in the responsibilities. How far did the position and the activities of the ordinary women in the cultus differ from that of the ordinary man?

The blessings which Israel received by virtue of her special relationship with God were many and varied, but were in the main concerned with long life, well-being, children, and land.[81] Women are therefore vital to the fulfilment of the promise, and there is no reason to suppose that they are in any way excluded from the blessings involved in being the people of God. 'It seems clear that the law was not designed to deprive women of the blessings of the cult. She was to share in the Sabbath rest, Exodus 20:8, to benefit from the reading of the law, Deuteronomy 31:9–13, and to rejoice before Yahweh with the men.'[82]

It is true that women did not receive circumcision which was the outward sign of the covenant. This may be a symbolic expression of the fact that women were of secondary status from birth, 'second-class citizens'. However, it may be that circumcision was also a sign of function (it was certainly used this way sometimes in Egypt[83]), marking out the men as the ones who would represent their families before God. As Calvin says, 'Although God promised alike to males and females what he afterwards sanctioned by circumcision, he nevertheless consecrated, in one sex, the whole people to himself.'[84] Interpretation of Exodus 4:24–26, where Zipporah circumcises her son, is difficult; but there is no hint of any cultic disqualification from performing such an act. Women, in spite of not undergoing the rite of circumcision themselves, were nevertheless never seen as part of the despised and detested 'uncircumcised'.[85] Thus women's lack of circumcision is not seen as excluding them from the covenant, although it may indeed reflect their lower status in society. In fact, the passage in Genesis 17 where circumcision is introduced as a covenant sign is interrupted by the special mention of the blessing on Sarah.

The responsibilities of the people of Israel and their worship are seen in:

a. *Keeping the law.*   The Israelite woman was responsible equally with the man for keeping the law and maintaining the purity of the culture. The law was read aloud to both men and women, 'that they may hear, and learn to fear the Lord your God and be careful to do all the words of this law'.[86] Both men and women were to be

put to death if they did not 'seek the Lord ... with all their heart'
themselves, thus transgressing the law[87], or if they led others
astray.[88]

b. *Sacrifices and gifts.*   The majority of sacrifices were brought by
males as the representatives of their household, but Leviticus 12:6
and 15:29 show that women were expected to take an independent
role in bringing sacrifices.[89] 'Whenever a sacrifice was required of
an individual, no evidence has been found which would cause us to
doubt that if that individual was a woman she was expected to fulfil
personally this requirement.'[90] That the law made specific provision
for even 'non-contagious' types of uncleanness in women shows
that their personal cultic condition was a matter for concern.
There is no record of a woman actually bringing one of these
prescribed sacrifices, but no reason to suppose that they did not do
so. Women are described as participating personally in some way
in two sacrifices in the Old Testament. In Judges 13:15f Manoah
and his wife bring an offering, and in 1 Samuel 1:24f the major part
in bringing the sacrifice seems to be played by Hannah in spite of
the fact that Elkanah was present.

In the case of gifts, in all cases where gifts were brought individually rather than by families, for example in the equipping of the
tabernacle[91], both men and women were freely able to bring.

c. *Attending feasts.*   All Israelite males were required by the law
to 'appear before the Lord' three times a year at the major feasts.[92]
The women were not under any such obligation. There is no
explanation given as to why they were not, though it seems likely
that it was for reasons of their responsibilities at home and their
frequent ritual uncleanness.[93] There is certainly no law which
would prevent the women from attending the feasts if they so
desired. That they sometimes did so appears to be fairly certain.[94]

d. *Prayers and vows.*   In the Old Testament women are presented
as being able to come before God in just the same way as the men.
Their being under the authority of their husband or father did not
mean that they were removed from Yahweh. Several women are
mentioned as praying,[95] although Hannah's is the only personal
prayer which is itself recorded. The women could enquire of God
through the prophets, directly and independently of their husbands; this is shown in the cases of Rebekah, Genesis 22:22, and
Jeroboam's wife, 1 Kings 14:1. Hagar, Genesis 16:17, and
Manoah's wife, Judges 13:3, were spoken to directly by the angel of
the Lord. Nowhere is the husband presented as a necessary
mediator between his wife and God.

As far as the vows of a woman are concerned, they could always be cancelled by her husband or her father, but if they were not so cancelled, then the woman was as responsible as a man for fulfilling the vow. Vos points out that if we compare the elements involved with a vow, such as cleansing regulations, then 'the Nazirite vow . . . brought one in some respects to the level of consecration of a high priest.' It is particularly noteworthy therefore, that both men and women were equally eligible to take this vow.[96]

e. *Sanctuary worship, singing and dancing.* Sanctuary worship in Old Testament times did not take the form of the worship services that we know today, but it played an important part in the life of Israel, not only at the great feasts when everybody came together, but also at other times. There is no evidence that any restrictions were placed on women in worship. There is no sign of any problem about Hannah approaching the sanctuary (1 Samuel 1). Women are recorded as ministering at the door of the tent of meeting. It is not quite clear what form this ministry took, but it does appear to have played some part in the cult.[97] The Shunamite woman attended some form of worship with Elijah on Sabbaths and new moons (2 Kings 4:23). Singing and dancing are not always cultic, and, in fact, 'there is no clear reference to legitimate cultic dancing after the time of David'.[98] However, when it did occur, women played an important though not an exclusive role.[99] Women are recorded as singing in worship, as individuals, as a group, and as part of a mixed 'choir' which probably took some part in the worship of the temple.[100]

The law recognized the social structure of the time and accepts the husband as the leader of the family, yet it is remarkable how little this leadership factor comes into the picture while the woman is at worship. Elkanah is clearly seen as the head of his family and as their cultic representative, but nevertheless Hannah can as an independent being, pray, vow, name the child, decide to remain at home until the child was weaned, bring a sacrifice, present the child, and pray a psalm of praise. It is important to note that the restrictions on the worship of women and the introduction of a separate, lower court of the women can nowhere be found in the Old Testament, but are 'an intertestamental and unbiblical innovation that developed out of corrupted Judaism'.[101]

Woman in Office

'In the theocracy of Israel, woman had in fact a position of equality before God which was unique in the cultural patterns of the Ancient Near East. Women held every office in Hebrew society; prophetess (2 Kings 22:14; Nehemiah 6:14), judge (Judges 4:4), and even queen (though a wicked usurper, 2 Kings 11:3).'[102] Payne's statement here is quite true, but it does not give a complete picture of the situation. Jacob is probably more realistic when he says, 'The Old Testament always assigns the woman the inferior role, in the religious domain as well as in social life, though this does not prevent her from fulfilling on occasions the functions of military leader or prophetess; but generally the place of the woman is in the home....'[103] However, women, even in the androcentric Israelite society, did take office, and we must enquire how far they were able to exercise leadership.

The official leadership of the cult was in the hands of the priesthood, and, unlike other religions of the Ancient Near East, there were no priestesses at all in Israel. It had been suggested that this was to avoid the dangers of the fertility cults and sacred prostitution. The ineligibility of women to become priests may have been because most women started a family at about sixteen, because of regular ritual uncleanness, or because of the heavy work involved in moving dead animals, etc. The reason can be only conjecture, the fact remains that although the women of priestly families were given certain privileges,[104] they were never given the opportunity of becoming priests. It should perhaps be pointed out that it was not men as opposed to women who were eligible to be priests, but male descendants of Aaron as opposed to all other Israelites, men or women.

The term prophetess may at times have been used as an honorary title, as possibly in Isaiah 8:3, but there is no doubt at all that there were women who exercised a very real prophetic ministry. Calvin was of the opinion that prophetesses arose, 'whenever God wishes to brand man with a mark of ignominy'. Of Deborah and Huldah he says, 'God doubtless wished to raise them on high to shame the men,' and he thought that the prophesying of Miriam 'never ceased to be a reproach to her brother'.[105] It is difficult to find the evidence on which he based these views, for as Vos says, 'The Old Testament does not depict the appearing of prophetesses as an emergency measure.'[106] There may have been no suitable men available at the time of Deborah when she exercised leadership in political, military, civil and religious spheres (Judges 4), although this is difficult to believe, but in the time of Huldah[107] it is certainly not true, for both Jeremiah and Zephaniah were active at this time. As far as Huldah is concerned, five men who were themselves national leaders went to her without apparent debate, for advice as to the instructions of the Lord concerning the book of the law which Josiah had found. This 'is a strong indication that in this period of Israel's history there was little if any prejudice against a woman uttering a prophecy'.[108]

There were false female prophets,[109] just as there were false male prophets. They are condemned for their false prophecy but nowhere is there any hint of condemnation for prophesying as women. The existence of female prophets is an indication of the considerable religious influence that could be exerted by women. Joel 2:28f shows that in the future the gifts of prophecy were expected to be more widespread and to be given to both sexes indiscriminately.

The 'wise', whom Jacob describes as 'a special class, distinct from prophets and priests,... who by their counsel have an active influence on the course of events,'[110] were often women.[111] In exceptional cases, like Deborah and Athaliah, women undertook political leadership. Proverbs 31:1 indicates that a woman, especially as a mother, could speak and teach with authority.

Thus we have a double-sided picture of the leadership of women in the Old Testament. Women leaders were few and far between. The proportion of female to male prophets is very small and no writing prophets were women. Women were not eligible for the priesthood. But, on the other hand, there is no indication that women were ineligible for or incapable of leadership or authority. That women leaders did exist in a society where women were generally considered inferior is significant. As Vos puts it, 'One may not posit on the basis of the Old Testament, that when a woman functions in an official capacity her performance as an official is inferior to the performance of a man.'[112] There is also no indication in the Old Testament that the leadership of women over men is somehow alien to their created nature.

3. OLD TESTAMENT : CONCLUSION

Even a cursory reading of almost any section of the Old Testament immediately makes obvious the intensely androcentric nature of the society in which it was produced and with which it deals. It was a male orientated and male dominated society. The story revolves round the patriarchs, sons not daughters are important, religious ceremonies and even the law are largely geared to the male. Given this androcentricity, there are two questions for us to consider. Firstly, is the androcentricity complete? Is Kate Millett right to assert that 'Patriarchy has God on its side'?[113] Secondly, does this male-centred pattern of the Old Testament mean that androcentricity is therefore a God-ordained and inviolable concept?

In the Old Testament as a whole, woman, after the Fall, is seen as secondary. Even though Deuteronomy 29:9–18 makes it clear that she is a full member of the covenant community who must assume full responsibility for playing her part in it, nevertheless she is placed low down the order of those who are described as entering the covenant. She is seen as relative to a man, whether her husband or her father, and generally subject to him. However, when we consider all that the Old Testament has to say about women, it is clear that the androcentricity is not total, that patriarchy cannot accurately be described as having 'God on its side' and that just because androcentricity is recognized as existing, it cannot from the Old Testament be defended as a 'God-ordained and inviolable concept'. Women were full members of the covenant community. They had a significant role to play in the life of the nation, not only in their role as mothers and in the home, but also as individuals, and they were not barred from leadership when the circumstances required it. Similarly, the Old Testament is concerned with the personal relationship of women to God. As Trible expresses it, 'I know that Hebrew literature comes from a male dominated society. I know that biblical religion is patriarchal and I understand the adverse effects of that religion for women. I know also the dangers of eisegesis. Nevertheless, I affirm that the intentionality of biblical faith as distinguished from a general description of biblical religion is neither to create nor to perpetuate patriarchy, but rather to function as salvation for both men and women.'[114]

2

Contemporary Cultural and Religious Influences

1. JUDAISM

It is not easy to get a clear picture of the ideas or behaviour patterns of the Judaism of the time of Christ, regarding women. There is much information to be gained from the comments of the Rabbis in the Talmud, but it must be remembered that, although much material from earlier times is recorded, it was not until the fifth century AD, well after the time of Christ, that the Talmud was completed. Also, the written material, like that from more contemporary authors such as Josephus and Philo, reflects the particular point of view of the authors and does not therefore necessarily give a complete indication of the way of life of the ordinary people. Nevertheless, certain assumptions can be made from the evidence that is available, which points very strongly to the fact that first century Judaism made explicit the lower status of women.

The general Rabbinic view of women has been described as 'half kindly, half oriental',[1] and is accurately assessed by the fact that women are repeatedly linked with children and slaves. There are occasions where women are described as hardworking, compassionate or intelligent,[2] but they are more often seen as lazy, stupid, garrulous, vain, having a tendency to the occult,[3] and in many ways, frivolous and unteachable.[4] Jeremias points out that disdainful opinions far outweigh those of high esteem,[5] and the picture is well summed up by Josephus, when he says, 'The woman . . . is in all things inferior to a man.'[6]

There is a very high regard for marriage in Judaism, partly

because it was the means of propagating the Holy People and of ensuring a man's future in his offspring and partly because 'the family is regarded...as a religious institution to foster ideals of holiness.'[7] It was considered to be essential for a man to marry, and it was the unmarried rather than the married who were seen as unchaste.[8] Polygamy[9] and divorce[10] were both permitted fairly easily, but, largely because of economic reasons, they were not as common as might have been supposed. However, Jeremias sees their availability and the fact that the right to divorce was exclusively the husbands', as being key factors in affecting the status of women.[11] There was a rigorous condemnation of irregularity of sexual behaviour, but Bailey suggests that this did not really affect the double standard of morality which was heavily weighted on the side of the male.[12]

The sphere of women was regarded as exclusively domestic. Within that sphere, 'her position has always been one of unchallenged dignity,'[13] and she is honoured both as wife and as mother. Thus, 'in her place' the worth of the woman is clearly recognised, but even in the home she was very much under authority.[14] 'Josephus and the Talmud agree in saying that the wife is controlled by her husband's will.'[15] Philo considers wives to be 'in servitude to their husbands, a servitude...promoting obedience in all things'.[16] The 'acquisition' of a wife is compared with that of a Gentile slave. A man had a duty to 'feed, clothe and maintain' his wife, whereas, 'the wife's duty was to carry out the household tasks, and to wash her husband's feet, a task which the slaves could not be compelled to do.'[17] In practice, the home was a centre of community life and the women did have a certain amount of influence. Also in practice, wives were often very much more than simply housekeepers and child-bearers. As Ecclesiasticus puts it, a man's wife is 'a helper that suits him and a pillar to lean on' and above both a friend and a companion.[18]

Because the place of women was seen as totally within the home, her role in any sort of public activity, being outside the home, was automatically passive. In fact, as far as possible, women were expected to keep out of the public eye and preferably not to leave the house at all. Philo suggests that, 'women are best suited to the indoor life which never strays from the house,'[19] and the Talmud sees Psalm 45:14, 'The king's daughter is all glorious within', as a description of the restricted life of women never leaving their apartments.[20] However, only rich families could possibly afford total seclusion of this kind; wives generally had to help their husbands in their work, maybe selling their wares.[21] In any case, members of royal households made their own rules and were often far from secluded.[22] Edersheim is of the opinion that the New Testament indicates that the separation of women was not common and that in fact, 'woman mingles freely with others both at home and abroad.'[23] Perhaps custom varied, as in the case of veils, where, in Jerusalem, all women who went out were veiled, but this was probably not so in the country, where the rules were less vigorously upheld.[24]

Jewish writings reveal 'that the attempt was made to avoid the lustful glance by the greatest possible limitation of opportunities to meet with the opposite sex'.[25] Men were largely seen as innocents being seduced by wicked women.[26] This had a great effect on the life of women, particularly outside the home. The suggestion, 'Do not converse much with women as this will ultimately lead you to unchastity',[27] is repeated several times in the Talmud in various ways, and is applied even to a man's wife. That it was taken seriously is shown by the surprise of the disciples when they found Jesus discussing with a woman.[28] The education of women in Greece and Rome brought them into close contact with men and had led to lax moral behaviour. Perhaps for this reason Jewish schools were open only to boys and men. Women could gain merit only 'by sending their sons to learn in the synagogue and their husbands to study in the schools of the Rabbis and by waiting for their husbands until they return from the school of the Rabbis'.[29] It is possible that in wealthier families, girls were taught at home, perhaps to read, or even where Hellenistic ideas were acceptable, to speak Greek,[30] but in general, women learned only the domestic arts and were not thought capable of much more than this.[31]

In the courts the testimony of women bore very little weight.[32] Where their evidence was acceptable, so also was that of a Gentile slave.[33] The reason for this appears to be that Genesis 18:15, where Sarah denies having laughed, was interpreted as indicating that woman was by nature a liar.[34] As Josephus expressed it, 'From women let no evidence be accepted because of the levity and temerity of their sex.'[35]

The inferiority of women extended to the religious sphere also. Women were expected to be present at the seven year reading of the law, they were permitted to say the eighteen benedictions and there are records of women giving extempore prayer.[36] Women could together form the quorum of three necessary for saying grace, but if a man was present, 'a hundred women are no better than two men.'[37] At the Temple and in the synagogue, the general attitude was that 'the man came...to learn, the woman came to hear.'[38] Women were allowed into the Temple precincts only as far as the court of the women. They did not count at all for the quorum of ten necessary for a synagogue service to be held; thus women on their own could never hold an official service. Although theoretically they were permitted to be among the seven who read, 'this was disapproved of on the grounds of propriety... and... no instance is reported.'[39] The women could, in fact, take no active part at all in the synagogue service.

It is generally assumed that women and men sat separately in the synagogue, but the actual evidence for this is very slight. In the Temple, there were galleries erected for the women at the feast of tabernacles, perhaps 'as a precaution against the kind of "levity" to which the enthusiasm of the hour incited'.[40] Similar galleries are found in synagogues from the third century AD, but there is no evidence for them occurring earlier than this.[41] However, it is likely that the building of galleries with a separate entrance only made total a separation which had already existed for a long time. As Schurer puts it, 'the separation of the sexes must be assumed as self-evident, although it does not happen to be mentioned in any of the more ancient authorities, ... nor is a special division for women mentioned in the Talmud.'[42]

There are three extant tomb inscriptions from the Roman Jewish community with the title 'mater synagogue', compared with nine of 'pater synagogue'.[43] This is probably an honorary title perhaps indicating financial support, but it may be significant and does show that we must beware of dismissing the Jewish women as of no account in the synagogue.

The Talmud presents us with conflicting opinions regarding how much religious education should be given to women. Sot. 3:4 says, 'a man is obliged to have his daughter taught Torah', but this is immediately followed by 'whoever teaches his daughter Torah is as though he taught her obscenities,' and the overwhelming weight of opinion would seem to support the view of the latter; as 'let the words of the Torah rather be destroyed by fire than imparted to woman.'[44] It was not usual therefore for women to be educated at all; 'a woman has no learning except in the use of the spindle.'[45] However, there were exceptions to this, probably the most notable being Beruriah the daughter of Rabbi Hannina ben Teradion and the wife of Rabbi Meir. She is quoted as an illustration of wide scholarship;[46] and she even gave opinions on points of law, on one occasion her decision being approved, 'even though it went counter to the prevailing opinion of the learned'.[47]

As far as first century Judaism in general is concerned there is no doubt at all that the place of the woman was not equal to that of the man.[48] Women were subordinate and inferior to men in religion, in the society in general and also in the home and family. There were exceptions, the practice did not always follow the theory, the country was rather more free than the town and the lot of women in Judaism was still somewhat happier than that of women elsewhere in the Orient. But, nevertheless, it is possible to see a dramatic decline in the position and status of women in every sphere as compared to the situation as described in the Old Testament.

2. ESSENES AND THE QUMRAN SECT

We must beware of building up from the various sources too structured a picture of the attitude of these sects to women. H. F. D. Sparks warns us of the danger of assuming that all of the scrolls found at Qumran were 'produced' rather than just 'possessed' by the Qumran community[49], and C. Roth presents strong arguments against the Qumran sectaries being Essenes.[50] Nevertheless, we do have clear evidence, both in the case of the Essenes and of those at Qumran, that they were sects whose views of the position of women were even more rigid than that of Judaism in general.

Philo,[51] Josephus,[52] and Pliny,[53] all make it clear that the Essenes in general did not marry. Pliny described them as 'a solitary tribe...which is remarkable above all other tribes in the whole world, as it has no women, and has renounced all sexual desires'. However, Josephus tells us also that there was 'another order of Essenes' who did marry, although solely for the purpose of procreation.[54] Lohse points out that their abstention from marriage was not so much from a tendency to asceticism, which would have been foreign to Judaism, but rather that they might not be made unclean by association with a wife.[55] It was not that they were misogynists as such, but that apart from procreation women were considered to be irrelevant.

At Qumran too, women appear to have been considered largely irrelevant. The Rule of Community, 1 QS, 'is clearly a rule for an all male militarily ordered society'.[56] It contains no material concerning relations between men and women, nor anything, even in the section dealing with discipline, about sexual offences. However, the Rule of the Congregation, 1 QSa, looks forward to a time when the whole of Israel will be properly regulated and the women as well as the men will come to listen to the exposition of the law.[57] It also specifies the correct age for marriage and sex,[58] and, 'probably, though the translation is disputed, provides for the admission of wives to the lowest stage of adult participation in the meetings of the community'.[59] Certainly the graves of a small number of women and children have been found near the Qumran burial ground.

The Damascus Rule, CD, forbids sexual intercourse 'in the city of the sanctuary', but provides for marriage for 'those who live in camps'.[60] It is nowhere explicitly stated that full initiation necessarily involved celibacy. Bruce sums up the situation when he says, 'While the evidence is inconclusive, it is conceivable that those adherents of the community who lived in the towns and villages of Judea...married and brought up children in the usual way... whereas those who lived in the wilderness as full members... denied themselves these comforts and responsibilities, looking on them as encumbrances for men involved in the "militia dei".'[61]

The fact that they saw themselves as an army preparing to fight a religious war, largely explains the reason why they considered women to be irrelevant. It was inconceivable that women would have any active role to play in that situation, and as it was essential for the men to keep themselves ready for war, and therefore separate from women, the role of the woman as wife and mother was not applicable either. That their view of women was not entirely negative comes out in their strong condemnation of polygamy, seen as a curse of Israel[62], and by comments such as 'no husband shall cancel an oath without knowing whether it should be kept or not.'[63] That is, he should cancel the oath of his wife only if to keep it would have meant a transgression of the law. However, in general it must be acknowledged that there was no place for women in their community.

3. THE GRAECO-ROMAN WORLD

The world of the Roman Empire during the first century AD was socially and culturally in a state of flux. Two very different cultures had come together, and as a result of this and other factors, 'standards of public and social life had changed considerably.'[64] It is not easy to obtain a complete picture of the role of and the attitude to women in these times. Over such a wide geographical and ethnic area there were obviously variations. In any case, most of the evidence that we do have concerns noble or royal women, not those from ordinary families. As Woolf puts it, 'When one attempts to make a sketch of the women...of the lower middle and proletariat classes in the Roman Empire, the direct notices at our disposal are meagre.'[65] It is possible to build up a general view of the situation, but in order to get an impression of the somewhat hectic atmosphere of the times, we must look briefly at the situation in Greek and Roman society before so many changes came so quickly, and consider what effect such changes had.

In ancient Greece, 'women were little more than chattels'.[66] They were 'regarded primarily as a means of producing healthy and efficient citizens',[67] 'regarded as a means not an end and... treated in a manner consonant with this view'.[68] Women were seen as essentially inferior to men, as belonging 'by nature to a lower genus than men'.[69] Greeks, unlike Jews, had no concern for moral purity; prostitution, homosexuality, etcetera, were widely tolerated, and sometimes institutionalized.[70] It is true that the Greek philosophers tended to affirm equality in principle, based on the philosophical ideal of the unity of reality, but apart from the Epicureans, where women participated on a fully equal basis, it was 'hardly ever actualised in practice'.[71]

The Roman view of marriage was higher than the Greek. The Roman mother 'enjoyed an exceptional dignity, freedom and equality with her husband. Nevertheless, her essential subservience and dependent status was reflected and defined in the legal doctrine of the 'patria potestas'.[72] That is, she was under the 'manus' or authority of her husband. Moral purity, though by no means always adhered to, was seen as a virtue and there was in some spheres a tendency towards puritanism.

However, in the changing situation leading up to the first century AD, as a result of various factors such as the mixing of cultures, the increasing wealth which was available as the Empire developed, and the growing influence of certain queens and other noble women, two developments arose which are relevant for our purposes. One was the changing attitude towards women, leading to an increased emancipation, and the other was a marked decline in standards of morality.

The general status of women had improved over a long period of time. Now, 'the traditional absolutism of the "patria potestas" was attenuated.'[73] The economic rights of women over such things as inheritance, ownership of property, and their rights in divorce, were increased. Marriages between different classes became more common. There were several women of outstanding accomplishment in art and literature, such as Agrippa, Sulpicia, Balbilla, and the wife of Pliny, so much so that Seneca was able to suggest that women had an equal capacity for culture with men.[74] Women began to accompany their husbands on political missions, as did, for example, the wives of Pilate and Agrippa. They became more influential in the organization of the life of the towns and even in the administration of provinces. 'Women now received citizenship and proxeny from other cities for the same services as men; and the women magistrates of the Roman period date back at any rate to the first century BC when a woman, Phile, held the highest office at Priene and built a new aqueduct and reservoir.'[75] Freedom was therefore available to women, but in reality only to those who could grasp their opportunities. The extent of emancipation must not be exaggerated. Most women were still considered to be very much inferior to and remained under the dominance of their husbands, though the fact that wives were now able to control their own property, acquired by dowry or legacy, meant that they could have at least a measure of independence.

The changing of traditional social roles was certainly not accepted by all. Some deliberately violated old traditions, but others as vigorously defended them. 'Among those who advocated preservation of the status quo, the constantly salient concern is a sense of order.... The differentiation and ranking of women and men became a potent symbol for the stability of the world order. That concern comes through clearly, for example, in the protestations by moralists about the "natural" difference in hair styles for men and women.'[76]

Alongside the gradual emancipation of women was a parallel tendency towards moral laxity. It would be wrong to link the two directly because there is no doubt that many other factors were involved, but certainly both were important factors in the social life of that age. Bailey points out that while the greater social freedom 'ameliorated the lot of Greek women and tended to transform for the better the character of Greek marriage, in Rome it had the opposite effect.' Women could now evade the restrictions of 'manus', 'but this served only to hasten a general moral decline which was marked by the growing prevalence of divorce and the disintegration of family life.'[77] As the influence of women increased, marriages for political reasons became more common. Often these did not last long and some members of the aristocracy were married as often as four or five times. Gradually, 'the baser elements of Greek sexual life undermined the severe puritanism of the earlier tradition,' and 'the spontaneous naturalism of Greek sensuality' in Rome became 'brutal calculated vice'.[78] Many Roman nobles did retain a high standard, but 'corruption and provincial maladministration increased as a more luxurious and ostentatious standard was set by fashion.'[79]

Thus there was a steady decline of morality on the part of the governing classes. However, although the decline was marked, and influenced the attitude of the whole of society, its extent must not be over-estimated. 'It is easy to draw an unpleasant picture of the Roman aristocracy...of luxury, vulgar ostentation...and licence...but exaggeration must be avoided. Demoralization was largely limited to the governing class.'[80] Poorer homes, often governed by the economic necessities of everyday living, tended to be much more stable, and in certain areas of the Empire, family life continued to be normal and healthy.

Alongside the moral laxity of the times was the ascetical ideal of the philosophers. This mostly grew out of the pessimistic dualism where all material things were seen as evil, but it was partly a reaction against the ugliness of the moral laxity, and 'in its sexual aspect was partly due also to the low contemporary view of women and marriage'.[81] The Stoics sought to be totally self-sufficient and therefore tended to reject all family ties including marriage. The Neo-Pythagoreans inclined towards 'a dualism which regarded coitus as a defilement and inculcated continence'.[82]

Thus we are left with a picture of a very varied society with an atmosphere that in this area can truly be described as 'hectic'.[83] In general there was still a low opinion of the value of women, for although in theory the first century Gentile view was similar to that of Judaism, 'in practice it was content with a much lower standard, and at best rarely succeeded in realizing even its own ideals.'[84] Emancipation was taking place, but was largely restricted to the wealthier classes, and even there did not go unopposed. The standards of morality, again particularly in the upper classes, were very low with sexual behaviour being particularly lax. It was in this sort of atmosphere that most of the churches whose origins are described in the New Testament grew up.

4. CONTEMPORARY INFLUENCES : CONCLUSION

In the early years of the Christian Church, the gospel was preached and the books of the New Testament were written, in the context of a particular environment. In order to understand and interpret the New Testament, we must have some appreciation of that environment. For, although it would be wrong to suggest that the shape of the gospel was totally determined by environment, as this is manifestly not true, nevertheless the environment did have both a positive and a negative influence on the theological ideas and practices of the New Testament church.

The negative influence is seen in the reaction against those ideas and philosophers which were felt to be incompatible with the teaching of the gospel. Paul's thought, for example, seems on occasion to be formulated in response to certain heretical ideas which were creeping into the newly founded churches. Also, just as the excesses of the Canaanites served as an 'awful warning' to the Old Testament community, so the New Testament writers reacted strongly against the excesses and the heathen practices which were so prevalent in their time.

In a more positive way, the New Testament is deeply influenced by the Old. The writers were in general, steeped in Old Testament thought, and constantly used the Old Testament to support and to interpret new ideas. In addition to this, it is inevitable that the writers, living in a particular cultural milieu, would be steeped in the concepts and conventions of their time which would thus govern the pattern of their thought and the meaning of their terminology.

D. S. Bailey lists three separate ways in which the ideas of the primitive church concerning the relation of the sexes were influenced by the background environment.[85]

i) The Jewish respect for marriage and the family led to the 'ideal of the Christian home as in some senses a religious institution'.

ii) The ascetical ideal of the philosophies led to the view of post New Testament times that sex was somehow evil, and probably influenced the way in which such chapters as 1 Corinthians 7 were interpreted.

iii) As far as the general attitude to women and marriage is concerned the early Christians were children of their time. They submitted to the 'common civil law by which the status of women was defined', that is, to Roman law, and in all material respects they 'conformed to the established conventions which governed the social intercourse between the sexes'.

However, it is important to note that while these factors did influence New Testament thought and practice they did not control its development. 'The Christian sexual tradition did not originate merely in a synthesis of elements derived from Judaism on the one hand and from Hellenistic asceticism on the other.'[86] As W. D. Davies puts it when he discusses the way in which the worship of the early Christians was influenced by the synagogue, the church 'manipulated traditional forms freely, and experimented not only with... but often... in defiance of them. Thus although rooted in the synagogue tradition the church allowed women to pray and prophesy.'[87]

In considering the teaching and the practice of the New Testament, we shall look at many examples of the influence of their background on the writers, as it is only in considering particular examples that the extent of such influence can be seen. Suffice it to say here that if we are to understand what the writers of the New Testament meant and how their original readers would have understood what they said, it is essential that we first know something of the thought and practice of the cultural environment in which they lived.

3

The Gospels

1. GOSPELS : INTRODUCTION

To turn from a consideration of the place of women in Judaism and in the Roman Empire of New Testament times to look at the attitude and behaviour of Jesus as presented in the gospels, is to be immediately aware of a startling contrast. Jesus' approach to women is 'without precedent in contemporary Judaism'.[1] Jeremias, in considering the impact of the Kingdom of God in the life of the believer says of the place of women, 'Nowhere in the social sphere does the new life make so striking an incursion into everyday affairs as here.'[2] Jesus healed women, he allowed them to touch him and to follow him; he spoke without restraint of women, to women and with women. He related to women primarily as human beings rather than as sexual beings, that is, he was interested in them as persons, seeing their sex as an integral part but by no means the totality of their personality.

Jesus' attitude to women comes across clearly in every source and in every form; parables, miracle stories, discourses, etc., all lead us to the same conclusion. Luke is often presented[3] as the gospel writer who has a particular concern to present Jesus as caring for women and it is true that Luke notes several incidents concerning women that are not related by the other gospels.[4] Nevertheless, all the synoptic gospels, and John as well[5], present us with the same picture of Jesus as one who not only showed concern for the well being of women but gave them their true worth and took note of their ideas and opinions whether he accepted[6] or rejected[7] these. As Moule puts it, 'All the quite varied traditions in

44

all four gospels tell the same story.'[8] That this is so in spite of the fact that the contemporary view was so different[9], is quite remarkable and shows something of the significance that the gospel writers attributed to this aspect of the life and character of Jesus.

So, from the gospel accounts a portrait of Jesus emerges which is 'clear and consistent.... His attitude to women was startlingly new, he was able to mix freely and naturally with women of all sorts, and women followed and ministered to him.'[10] His approach can accurately be described as revolutionary, and we must take care in assessing the impact of Jesus' approach from our 'post-revolution' standpoint, not to forget just how revolutionary it was.

2. JESUS' APPROACH TO WOMEN

Women as Subjects not Objects

The key to an understanding of Jesus' attitude to women is perhaps to be found in Matthew 5:28, 'But I say to you that everyone who looks at a woman lustfully has already committed adultery with her in his heart.'[11] The fundamental dichotomy which exists between Jesus and the Rabbis on this issue, is not over the question of lust being sin – they were in complete agreement about that – but of lust being inevitable. To the Jews, if the sexes were to come into any kind of social contact, lust was unavoidable. As Jeremias puts it, 'The world of Jesus set out to protect women by secluding them, believing that sexual desire was uncontrollable.'[12] In fact, in Judaism, the woman was seen as a constant danger to the man and it is probably the men rather than the women who were seen as needing to be protected from danger, by the women being removed as far as possible from the public eye. The line of argument that advocated complete sexual segregation is perfectly logical and the restrictions sensible if one assumes, as the Rabbis tended to, that the primary function of women was to be man's sexual partner and that the automatic result of contact between the sexes would be lust.

However, Jesus, in contrast to the Rabbis, completely dismisses the suggestion that lust is inevitable. He does not warn his followers against looking at a woman, but against doing so with lust. Women are to be recognised as subjects in their own right, as fellow human beings, fellow disciples, and not just the objects of men's desire. Their life and rights are to be recognised as important and not to be endangered by the natural desires of the men.[13] Once it is recognised that women are people who can be related to in other ways than that of sexual desire, and once it is acknowledged that lust is not only sin but deliberate sin, as much an act of the will as is adultery, then there is no longer any necessity to avoid social contact. Therefore, 'Jesus accepts women into the group of disciples because he expects his disciples to control their desires.'[14]

In his teaching on divorce also, Jesus brings home the point that women are not objects to be dismissed at will. Rather he stresses that marriage is a God-ordained permanent partnership, and both the husband and the wife are responsible for keeping this partnership secure.[15] The concept of commiting adultery against one's wife is in itself an unusual one as the emphasis was more often on the offence against the husband of the other woman, and to suggest, as in Mark 10:12, that the woman could be responsible for divorcing her husband would have been unthinkable to the Rabbis. Jesus is, of course, not suggesting that such a thing ought to happen, but emphasising that loyalty and commitment in marriage is the responsibility of both partners.

The value Jesus gave to women is shown too in the way he talked about them. 'Leaving one's sister'[16] would not have been seen by Jews at the time of Christ as a sacrifice; for a sister was at best seen as a responsibility and more often as a burden. However, Jesus valued women enough to assume that leaving a sister would be as much a sacrifice as was leaving parents or children or houses. Similarly, in Luke 13:16 we have the description of the crippled woman as a 'daughter of Abraham'. 'Son of Abraham' was a commonly used title, particularly when the worth of a man as a member of the covenant community was being emphasised. But, possibly because women were generally thought of as related to their families rather than as citizens of the nation, the title 'daughter of Abraham' is virtually unknown in Judaistic writings. It appears that Jesus deliberately chose the title to bring out the value he placed on this woman.

Thus we are left with the clear impression that, to Jesus, the intrinsic value of women as persons is just as great as that of men, an idea found nowhere in, and in some ways alien to, the Jewish thought of the time. As we shall see, this attitude led to radical differences in the way that Jesus treated women, and also in the way that he expected his followers to treat women.

Women in Everyday Life

Jesus' strong condemnation of even looking lustfully, and probably also the severity of his teaching on divorce made it possible for women to mix freely with the group of disciples without their being immediately condemned as immoral persons. The addition made by Marcion[17] to Luke 23:2 where Jesus' association with women is introduced as part of the charges at his trial shows that 'Jesus' attitude to women and the fact that a group followed Jesus, did not pass unnoticed; it was seen as a distinctive feature of the ministry of Jesus which must have drawn the ire of his opponents.'[18] However, the fact that the religious leaders of the time took Jesus so seriously, asking complex theological questions in an attempt to trip him up, shows that these charges of misconduct in relationships between the sexes, if they did occur, were generally recognized to be false or at least to be unrelated to moral issues. If there had been the slightest evidence of sexual misbehaviour, then Jesus' ministry would have been discredited and there would have been no need for further investigations.

It is astonishing that in the society in which they lived, and with the strictness of his teaching on sexual matters, Jesus, while expecting this teaching to be firmly adhered to, also expected men and women to mix freely. Thus he confirms his conviction that social relations between the sexes and lustful desire are not automatically linked. Jesus himself totally ignored the rabbinic injunction to 'talk not much with women' and numbered many women among his friends and followers.

That Jesus had compassion for those who suffered, whether male or female, and that he healed women as well as men is not perhaps surprising. What is more surprising is that he completely ignored any injunctions against incurring legal or ritual impurity in order to do so. In the case of the woman with the flow of blood[19] Jesus deliberately called attention to the fact that she had touched him, which would automatically make him unclean[20], and yet, here, as on all other occasions when he healed or touched women, there is no indication that he felt it necessary to undergo the purification rites set out in the law. It is possible that his doing so is taken for granted, but this seems unlikely in view of the fact that he is specifically mentioned as not following other rabbinic cleansing rites.[21] This is probably an indication that in fulfilling the law Jesus makes purification rites of all kinds unnecessary, but it may have more significance regarding the place of women under the new covenant.

It is significant that not only did Jesus not hesitate to touch women, or to take them by the hand, even on the Sabbath,[22] but also he allowed women – even those recognised as being immoral – to touch him. The gospels present us with a 'strangely convincing picture of Jesus – a young unmarried man – allowing himself to be fondled and kissed by such women, without either embarrassment or aquiescence in their morals'.[23] He showed that it was possible for men and women to relate as human beings, even as different sexes, without any of what D. S. Bailey describes as the venereal aspects of sex[24] entering into that relationship.

Jesus not only spoke freely with women, healed them, allowed them to touch him and to bring their children to see him, he also allowed them to serve him. This was not, of course, unusual in a family situation, but it was unusual for a Rabbi, as the Rabbis strongly disapproved of women even serving them at tables.[25]

Thus we see Jesus' radical approach to women lived out in his day to day life. The Rabbis generally assigned to women a very inferior place but there is no sign of this in the life and ministry of Jesus. On the contrary, he talked to women, cared for them, healed them, freely admitted them into fellowship and accepted their service.

Women used in Parables

Jesus' reference to women in the illustrations which he used in his teaching indicates further his general attitude to them. Rabbinic parables pointedly avoided mentioning women[26], but Jesus often told stories relating to the life of women. He spoke of using yeast in bread-making, of childbirth, of grinding meal, of wedding attendants, of housewives and of widows. He used pictures of women to illustrate themes of vigilance, of perseverance in prayer, of divine mercy and of the joy of God over the salvation of a lost sinner. The impression is gained that women were not, as the Rabbis seemed to imply, necessary but of only secondary significance; but rather that they were an integral part of the creation, both necessary and significant; seen as having worth as persons in their own right and not simply in relation to men.

Women as Responsible People

Although the approach of Jesus to women was radically new in his time, and although he elevated them to a position of equal worth with men, the gospels nowhere present us with an idealistic or romanticized picture of women. Like men, women are all sinners in need of forgiveness and they are presented as such. Like that of men, their sin needs to be dealt with and is never overlooked.

In the account of the woman taken in adultery[27], the hypocrisy of those who brought her is challenged by Jesus, but her sin is by no means condoned. She is not even told that her sins are forgiven, although this is perhaps implicit in Jesus' words to her; rather she is told to go and sin no more, thus giving proof of her repentance. She is dealt with, as a sinner, according to her needs. When the 'woman of the city, who was a sinner',[28] in an act of humility and love anointed Jesus' feet, he did not ignore the fact that she was a sinner, rather he openly acknowledged it and took the opportunity to deal with her sins. Similarly, in talking to the woman of Samaria[29], the facts of her sin and of her need are brought out into the open. Each of these women is seen as responsible for her own sin and as needing that sin to be forgiven.

Jesus showed that the opinions of women mattered, in a way that Judaism rarely acknowledged. He paid attention to what they said, listened and considered. He took them seriously enough to refute wrong ideas. As G. B. Caird comments on Luke 11:27–28 where a blessing is called on the mother of Jesus, 'The words of the woman in the crowd were a common form of extravagant compliment; but Jesus dismissed them as sheer sentimentality.'[30] That he bothered to comment at all brings out the importance to him of what the woman thought.[31]

Pope Paul VI towards the end of Vatican II described woman as 'a reflection of a beauty greater than herself, the sign of a goodness that appears to us as having no bounds. . . .'[32] The gospels know nothing of such an unrealistic picture. It is true that there is no record in the gospels of any woman opposing Jesus, but woman is by no means idealised. She is rather seen as responsible and rational, able to make decisions and responsible for the consequences of any decisions that she might make.

Women as Followers and Disciples

It was not unusual for women of means to make contributions towards the support of Rabbis. Luke 20:47 shows that this fact was sometimes taken advantage of by certain of the scribes. However, the Rabbis in general preferred to avoid as much as possible the company of even such women as these. The attitude of Jesus on the other hand, 'encouraged many women to take this very unusual step of following him and ministering to him'.[33] The gospels point out[34] that for a great part of the ministry of Jesus he was accompanied not only by the twelve apostles but also by several women, whose gratitude to him and love, led them to follow him.

It is almost impossible from the information given in the gospels to assess accurately when Jesus is teaching the twelve and when he is addressing the wider group of disciples. It is apparent that at times he is alone with the three, at other times alone with the twelve, and that on some occasions at least seventy accompanied him. However, Luke 8:1–2 in particular makes it clear that on many occasions when only the twelve are mentioned, the women must have been there as well. That the early church recognised this fact is shown by Origen when he emphasises that women went out into the wilderness with the apostles 'forgetting the weakness of their sex and a regard for outward propriety in thus following their Teacher into the desert places'.[35]

It has often been seen as significant that the twelve apostles were all men. It is a fact that although women fulfilled the conditions for apostleship as set out in Acts 1:21–22 there were no women among the twelve.[36] It is possible that this fact was meant to have permanent significance for the leadership of the Church. It is also possible to suggest that it has only a temporary significance. For in that particular cultural setting only males would have been acceptable both as the closest companions of Jesus and as leaders of the community which was to be formed, though certainly Jesus' actions elsewhere would indicate that he was quite willing and able to go against the normal cultural patterns if necessary. The appointment of twelve Jewish males clearly does have some significance particularly in the light of Luke 22:30 where there appears to be a parallel drawn between the twelve apostles and the patriarchs.[37] However, whether the fact of their being male has any greater, or any different, significance for the leadership of the future church community than the fact of their being Jewish is not made clear in the gospels.

Blum points out that unlike the twelve, the women who followed Jesus were not specially called and commissioned, but rather that they came in response to Jesus' help and healing.[38] This is true, though if, as seems not unlikely, some of the seventy who were sent out were women, then women too would have been chosen and appointed for this task.[39] Certainly the women at the tomb were sent out to proclaim the message of the resurrection, being given a 'quasi-apostolic role'.[40]

These women following Jesus were not 'passive spectators, they rendered service from their possessions'.[41] It is not clear exactly what form this service took, although obviously financial provision is included. Beyer[42] tells us that the word *diakonein* "to serve", 'has the special quality of indicating very personally the service rendered to another'. Matthew 25:42–44 shows that serving includes many different activities, such as providing hospitality or visiting those in need. 'The term thus comes to have the full sense of active Christian love for the neighbour and as such it is the mark of true discipleship of Jesus.'[43] In the Acts and in the epistles, prophecy (1 Peter 1:10–12), preaching (Acts 19:22), and collecting for the saints (2 Corinthians 8:19) are all seen as forms of service. It is likely that as well as paying for food the women prepared and served it, particularly as the original meaning of *diakonein* was 'to wait at table'.[44] That the woman also shared with the rest of the disciples in other activities such as their teaching sessions is indicated by such verses as Luke 10:39 and John 11:28.[45]

Women in Theological Conversation

Possibly the most revolutionary aspect of Jesus' approach to women is not that he associated freely with them and treated them as responsible human beings, not that he had women as friends and not that he allowed them to listen to his teaching; but rather that he taught them personally, indulging in theological conversation with them, encouraging and expecting a response. At the synagogue women were thought of as coming to listen rather than to learn. Jesus assumed that women were capable not only of learning and understanding, but also of engaging in debate. He wanted from women, not only an acceptance of religious beliefs but also a full appreciation of the significance of that acceptance.

The Syro-Phoenician Woman (Matthew 15:21–28; Mark 7:24–39).[46] It is an interesting fact that two of the longest recorded conversations that Jesus had with women were not with Jewish women who might have been expected to have some understanding of who he was and of the meaning of his message; but with a Samaritan and with the Syro-Phoenician woman from the region of Tyre. This woman, seeking healing for her daughter, followed Jesus along the highway until she got on the disciples' nerves and they begged Jesus to get rid of her. However, Jesus' attitude was very different; he saw her as an individual and dealt with her in the way that she needed. He did not send her away but rather talked with her. He tested her; his refusal to help was leading her on to faith. She could understand that Jesus' first responsibility was to Israel and that she therefore had no claim no him; but she wanted only a crumb and recognised that it was in his power to give it. Her reply showed intelligence and insight. Jesus rejoiced at her faith and granted her request. What is significant here is not that the woman was intelligent, but that Jesus talked with her and deliberately sought to bring out her capacity for understanding.

The Samaritan Woman (John 4:7–12). It was unusual for a Jew to have a conversation with a Samaritan. However, Bultmann points out that the disciples were amazed not so much because Jesus talked with a Samaritan, but because he talked with a woman.[47] Jesus not only asked the woman for a drink and not only passed the time of day with her, both unusual things in themselves; he also gave her important theological teaching which, by treating her seriously and by responding to her replies he brought her to understand, even from a very unpromising beginning.[48] Again Jesus saw the woman as an individual; he brought out and dealt with her specific problems. He saw her also as capable of spiritual discernment. The enthusiasm of the woman about what she had learned was so great that she went back to the village and many believed because of her word. R. Brown sees as significant the fact that the same expression occurs in Jesus' prayer for his disciples (John 17:20, 'I do not pray for these only but also for those who believe in me through their word.') 'The evangelist can describe both a woman and the (presumably male) disciples at the last supper as bearing witness to Jesus through preaching and thus bringing people to believe in him on the strength of their word.'[49] It is interesting to note that the teaching of John 4 about the nature of the gospel and the nature of God must have come to the disciples through this woman.

Mary and Martha (Luke 10:38–42; John 11:20–33). The best known picture of Jesus' teaching women is that of Luke 10:39 where Mary 'sat at the Lord's feet and listened to his teaching'. 'The picture is that of a Rabbi instructing his pupil. The extraordinary feature is that the pupil is a woman.'[50] This verse tells us that Jesus gave private teaching to a wider group than the twelve apostles and that this group included women. That Martha too was taught by Jesus although on this occasion she was too busy to listen is brought out in John 11, where Martha reveals understanding of some of the things she has been taught.[51] Jesus takes time to teach her more and to lead her on into further understanding. This time, even in her grief, Martha is ready to listen. It is interesting to note that the nearest equivalent in John's gospel to Peter's confession of Christ (Matthew 16:16), which was seen as significantly related to his position of leadership in the church, is found here on the lips of Martha, 'You are the Christ, the Son of God.'[52]

The Anointing of Jesus (Matthew 26:6–13; Mark 14:3–9; John 12:1–8).[53] The woman who anointed Jesus is identified by John as Mary of Bethany. The accounts of this event bear witness to the fact that the teaching Mary received had born fruit. Some would see in her action merely a beautiful expression of her love which Jesus then interpreted as having more significance than she realized.[54] Others, however, are of the opinion that Mary knew what she was doing.[55] Matthew 26:12 and Mark 14:8 do seem to imply that Mary – with far more theological insight than was shown on this occasion by the disciples – understood that Jesus was soon to die. Perhaps she even foresaw that there would be no opportunity then for her to use the ointment she had been saving for his burial. It may be reading a little too much into the text to say that 'Mary now realizes that Jesus has quite a unique relationship to life and death and that therefore it is as natural to anoint his living body, for he is even now the resurrection, as it would be later on to anoint his corpse,'[56] but this is not impossible. In any case, it is clear that Jesus rebukes the disciples for assuming that their spiritual understanding was greater than that of the woman, and shows them that in this case, the opposite was, in fact, true.

3. WOMEN IN THE PASSION NARRATIVES

The part played by women in the events described in the last chapters of all four gospels is considerable. Women were present at the crucifixion of Jesus and at his burial. They were the first to hear the news of the resurrection. Matthew, Mark and John all depict women as being the first to see the risen Jesus, although Luke appears to have Peter as the first actually to see the Lord.[57] Women were also the first to speak of the resurrection. As Cranfield puts it, 'One feature of all four gospels which goes a long way towards authenticating the story as a whole is the prominence of women; for this is a feature which the early Church would not be likely to invent.'[58]

Women are primarily presented in these accounts as witnesses. To the Jews, the evidence given by women was of no account.[59] The events of the crucifixion and resurrection make it quite clear that for Christians this can never be so. As Lane points out, the significance of the presence of the women at the cross is that 'The details of what took place could be substantiated by their testimony.'[60] It is noteworthy that a number of the factual details concerning the death, burial and resurrection of Jesus are known only through the testimony of women. The fact that the women are mentioned as observing the burial itself (Matthew 27:61), probably indicates a desire to combat any suggestion that they might have mistaken the tomb.

As well as being witnesses to the facts, women are presented as receivers of the message. Cranfield suggests that it is significant that it was not one of the Twelve who was the first to receive the news of the resurrection, and that 'those who in the providence of God were given the precedence over the apostles on this momentous occasion were women.'[61] This may be so, though it would be a mistake to over-emphasize the point as it is quite possible that the women received the message first simply because they happen to have been there first. If so, then what is being stressed is not any particular precedence being given to women, but simply their 'loyalty and love'[62] and the fact that 'the very persons who in general held a rather despised position...were in this instance more persevering than the disciples. This feature delineates the new position of women in the fellowship of Jesus.'[63] Hendriksen commenting on John 20:12[64] questions if the angels appeared to the women rather than the men as a reward for their greater love or as support for their weaker faith; he comes to the conclusion that we do not know. However, there is no real necessity to assume that one of these alternatives must be correct; it seems likely that the angels appeared to the women as the ones who were first at the tomb, and having corroborated the evidence there was no need for them to appear again.

Not only are women witnesses to the facts and receivers of the message, they are also called to pass on the message they have received. They are shown to be the first announcers of the resurrection gospel. Severian of Gabala, in an interpretation[65] of Mark 16:8 ('They said nothing to anyone because they were afraid') described by Cranfield as 'quaint', suggests that the women were silent because theirs is to hear and not to speak and to learn and not to teach. However, though Calvin may be correct when he says of this verse, 'Though they were resolved to obey the angel, still they had not the power to do so, if the Lord himself had not loosed their tongues,'[66] nevertheless, Luke 23:9 and John 20:2,18 make it clear that their silence was only very temporary; their tongues were unloosed and their message was proclaimed. The women might have been the first to receive the message of the resurrection because they were first at the tomb; they were the first proclaimers of it by the direct command of the angels and of Christ himself.[67]

Luke 24:10–11 ('It was Mary Magdalene and Joanna and Mary the mother of James and the other women with them who told this to the apostles; but these words seemed to them an idle tale, and they did not believe them') makes it clear that the disciples did not give credence to the words of the women concerning the resurrection. Mark 16:14 ('Afterward he appeared to the eleven themselves as they sat at table; and he upbraided them for their unbelief and hardness of heart, because they had not believed those who saw him after he had risen')[68] shows that they were rebuked for their unbelief. That the news had come via women was obviously no excuse for their 'unbelief and hardness of heart'. Women in the Christian community were to be recognized as being as capable as men of bearing witness and of conveying the message revealed to them by Christ. Luke 24:13–35 may also provide support for this. We are not given any information about the second of the travellers to Emmaus, but as it appears that the place where they stop is the home of both (v 29), it does seem reasonable to suggest that they might have been man and wife. If this is so, then both heard Jesus' teaching, and both conveyed it to the rest of the disciples (v 35).

It is not clear whether the gospel writers give so much space in the passion narratives to the activities of women deliberately in order to make a point, or whether they are merely recording the facts as they occurred. H. Anderson makes the suggestion that Mark, for example, writes to encourage the women of his own community to faithful discipleship.[69] It is clear that the women played a very important part in the recording of these events and that at that time, the women who followed Jesus showed a greater perseverance, a greater loyalty and possibly a greater faith than even the twelve apostles.

4. THE ATTITUDE OF THE DISCIPLES

The picture of Jesus' radically different approach to women has been preserved in the gospels in spite of an alien environment both in Judaism and in the early church. Moule points out that in the epistles, though there is 'a new concern for women and a new tenderness towards them', nevertheless Jesus' attitude is never quite reproduced, there still remains 'a measure of repressiveness and sometimes...an almost scornful attitude,' for 'even the more liberal and genial passage in 1 Peter 3:7 does not go very far towards a positive estimate of womankind.'[70]

In spite of their background, however, the gospel writers do succeed in presenting this picture of Jesus and in doing so they also give us a picture of the disciples struggling to move from a Jewish to a Christian view of women. The disciples asked Jesus to send away the Syro-Phoenician woman. They rebuked those, probably women, who brought children to Jesus (Matthew 19:13–14), though we have no evidence of their rebuking men who came (cf John 12:21–22). They reproached the woman who anointed Jesus (Mark 14:5), taking it for granted that her action was senseless. They were astounded when Jesus talked to the Samaritan woman by the well, but this time they did not like to question him about it. Perhaps they had learned enough by now to know that while Jesus did not always respect the conventions of the Rabbis, he did have good reasons for what he did.[71]

When the women came to the disciples after the resurrection, the disciples did not believe their story, but they did wonder about it (Luke 24:22–24), enough to take some action. At the stage when the gospels were written, they were still scarcely comprehending. However, the fact that the gospels were written, bringing out all these points, showing very clearly the revolutionary attitude and behaviour of Jesus and indeed the lack of understanding of the apostles, is in itself an indication that a measure of understanding had, at last, been reached.

5. THE GOSPELS : CONCLUSION

'There can be little doubt that in Jesus' attitude towards women we have a highly original and significant feature of his life and teaching.'[72] It is original in that it was radically different from all the views and attitudes of his time; it is significant in the effects that it must have on the lives of those, both men and women, who follow Jesus. Jesus treats women as human beings and as such, as having value. It is not so much that he raises women to the level of men, for he does not appear to view people as being on levels; rather he sees both men and women as persons, as responsible individuals, with individual needs, individual failings and individual gifts. Jesus gives very little teaching on women as such, because he never treats them as a class, all with the same characteristics and tendencies. In a similar way he gives very little teaching for or about males as a class.

Although Jesus in no way seeks to deny or diminish the distinction between the sexes – he emphasises their partnership in marriage – it is nevertheless difficult to find any difference in the approach of Jesus to women and to men.[73] Each person, whether male or female is seen as a sinner in need of repentance and in need of forgiveness. Men and women alike are capable of making decisions and are responsible for the results of those decisions. Men and women alike are capable of a spiritual understanding.

Men and women alike could talk to Jesus, could follow him, could be friends with him, could serve him, could love him. In spite of the fact that Jesus was a male, the gospels show us that even in everyday life, men and women could relate to him in the same way, or rather that he related to them in the same way.

It remains true that Jesus specifically appointed the twelve and that they are all male; although it is not clear what significance this was intended to have for the church.[74] Apart from this the only difference in the gospel presentation appears to be that there is no record of any woman ever opposing Jesus, and that women played a larger role in the crucifixion and resurrection narratives. It is doubtful whether either of these latter points has any permanent significance for the life of the church.

6. EXCURSUS : MARY THE MOTHER OF JESUS

Mary was given a unique part to play in the outworking of God's plan for the salvation of mankind. As the early church fathers put it, she was *theotokos*, the one who gave birth to the divine Son of God. The facts of the Incarnation and the virgin birth in which Mary played such a vital role are of tremendous significance for Christology. Similarly the attitude of the Church towards Mary has an important place in the study of church history and of the development of doctrines. However, our concern here is not to investigate these areas but rather to discover the relevance which, according to the New Testament, the position of Mary has for the life of the Church.

In his infancy narratives, Matthew tells us that Mary 'was found to be with child of the Holy Spirit,' and that she gave birth to Jesus in Bethlehem while she was still a virgin. Luke gives us more detail, telling us of the angel's announcement to Mary that the birth would take place, of Mary's response to this announcement, of the reaction of Elizabeth, of Mary's song and of the presentation of the baby Jesus in the Temple. Apart from these infancy narratives the gospels mention Mary only in the accounts of the boy Jesus discussing with the teachers in Jerusalem (Luke 3:41–51), of the miracle at Cana (John 2:1–11), of Mary coming with Jesus' brothers and asking for him (Matthew 12:46–50; Mark 3:31–34; Luke 8:21), and of Jesus' words from the cross that the beloved disciple was now to consider Mary as his own mother (John 19:26–27).

These passages bring to our attention three things about the significance of Mary. Firstly, 'as a human being and as a mother, she is a witness of his true humanity, but also of his origin from God.'[75] That is, Mary is a particularly significant witness of certain events in the life of Christ. Secondly, she is to be acknowledged as being blessed by God (Luke 1:42–58), and in her willing response and dedication of herself to the will of God, in her faith and in her obedience, she is an example to be honoured and imitated, as indeed are all 'those who through faith and patience inherit the promises' (Hebrews 6:12). H. Kung, while acknowledging that 'there is nothing unique...about Mary's faith, nor has she any special insights into the mysteries of God', describes her as 'the example and model of Christian faith'.[76] Thirdly the tremendous responsibility with which Mary was entrusted, the way in which her faith, her love and her growing understanding are described, and her stance alongside the rest as they awaited the coming of the promised Holy Spirit should perhaps be seen as indications of the new status which the coming of Mary's son brought to women.

In the only reference to Mary outside the gospels,[77] where the disciples are found at prayer 'together with the women and Mary the mother of Jesus and with his brothers' (Acts 1:14), though she is singled out for mention by name, she comes only after 'the women' and does not appear to have any particular precedence in the group. This point, together with the fact that the New Testament does not ever, either by implication or by definite assertion, build upon the story of Mary in the doctrines of Man, the doctrine of salvation or the doctrine of the Church, means that we must be very wary of asserting that Mary has any further significance, other than as a witness and an example.

If in the greeting of the angel to Mary, the word 'Rejoice' (Luke 1:28) can be seen as an allusion to Zephaniah 3:14–17 and Zechariah 9:9, where the 'Daughter of Zion' is told to rejoice, then it is just possible that Luke is presenting Mary 'as the daughter of Zion in the sense this expression had in the Old Testament, the personification of the people of God'.[78] However, the vagueness of the allusion and the lack of any other evidence makes this unlikely. J. McHugh argues that the idea of Mary as the daughter of Zion is in fact the central motif of Luke 1 and 2, for 'the notion of Mary as the ideal or prototype of the Christian believer, the faithful and lowly servant of the Lord, corresponds in every single detail with the Old Testament concept of the faithful daughter of Zion.'[79] However, while Acts 1:14 makes it clear that Mary was, or at least became, a Christian believer, and while in her 'modesty and humility, and the gentle readiness of her obedience to God'[80] she can be seen as an example to all believers, it is nevertheless difficult to find any indication that the New Testament intends Mary to be seen as the ideal or prototype believer any more than say Simeon, or Anna or Elizabeth.

It has sometimes been concluded from the fact that Mary was chosen to be the mother of Christ who was God Incarnate, perfect and without sin, that she must herself have been perfect,[81] or at least the most perfect woman who ever lived. It is universally admitted that it was necessary for Mary to be redeemed by her Son, but it is often taken as self-evident that her redemption would have to be the most perfect. Thus Rahner assumes that in God's election of Mary to be the mother of Christ 'is also included the choice of Mary as the Holy One, as she who has been most perfectly redeemed'.[82] This conclusion that the choice of Mary to be the mother of Jesus is in itself an indication that she must therefore be the ideal Christian, the 'ideal representative of the Christian community'[83] leads on fairly naturally to the various dogmas concerning Mary which the church, and in particular the Roman Catholic Church, later formulated. However, it is not in itself a logically necessary conclusion, and it is not a conclusion that is anywhere drawn by the New Testament writers.

It is true that in his gospel John does mention Mary at the beginning and at the end of the ministry of Jesus (John 2:1–11; 19:25–27), but to conclude that 'Mary is the prototype and exemplar of faith and that is why she stands at the beginning and end of the earthly manifestation of Jesus',[84] seems to be no more justifiable than to see Simon Peter in that way simply because he is mentioned as believing and as following Jesus in both John 1 and John 21. It is possible to interpret the account of the wedding at Cana so that Mary is, even at this early stage, seen as a believer standing alongside Jesus as over the rest,[85] but the whole emphasis is on Jesus and the significance of his hour, and cannot be taken as indicating Mary to be the ideal believer. Indeed, John 2:4, 'Woman, what have you to do with me?' may be deiberately included so as to show Jesus as dissociating himself from his mother's interests. If so, this would tie in with the other passages where Jesus shows that his family – including his mother – cannot be given any special priority amongst his people (Mark 10:29–30; Matthew 10:37; Luke 14:26).[86]

Similarly, in John 19, the account of Jesus leaving his mother in the care of the beloved disciple tells us more about Jesus than it does about Mary. If this disciple is a type of all who love Jesus, so that all these are 'summoned to look upon Mary as their mother, because her faith . . . is to be the pattern of their own',[87] then the teaching which culminated in 1964 with the declaration of Pope Paul VI that Mary is the 'Mother of the Church' has some foundation. But again there is no particular indication in the text that the incident is meant to be seen as symbolic and no hint of such a concept can be found elsewhere in the New Testament.

Nevertheless, while we would not accept that Mary is presented by the New Testament as the 'personification of the people of Israel', as the 'Mother of the Church', as the ideal believer who is 'most perfectly redeemed' or even as 'the ideal woman', her importance as a witness, and as an example to the church, and certainly the significance of her unique role as the mother of Jesus must not be understressed. She was certainly a 'blessed woman' and the example of her life and in particular of her willing acceptance of and obedience to the will of God is one that any Christian can be proud to follow.

4

Acts and Epistles : Doctrinal Teaching

There is a remarkable consistency and unity in the teaching given by Paul and the other New Testament writers to the different churches, and each individual church group is seen very much as part of the much larger whole. The complete Church is very definitely presented as being one Body. Nevertheless, each community has its own particular characteristics with individual patterns of worship and leadership. As Schweizer puts it, 'There is no such things as *the* New Testament church order. Even in New Testament times circumstances were very varied.'[1]

In order to discover what consistency and what diversity there is in the place accorded to women by the New Testament churches, we will look firstly at the doctrinal teaching given to the churches on the nature of womanhood and on the function of women within the community and then we will consider the practical outworking of this teaching in the day to day lives of the different groups.

As we approach this task, two initial difficulties must be noted. The first problem we have is in discovering when there is a particular reference to the husband/wife relationship and when a more general reference to men and women. The Greek has only one word *gune* to stand for both woman and wife and one word *aner* to stand for both man and husband. It is necessary to keep this fact in mind as we consider the various passages involved.

In the second place, there is the basic hermeneutical difficulty of relating the overall message to the specific teaching of individual passages. The former is obviously built up from the latter, but in coming to an understanding of the latter we are clearly and to some extent rightly influenced by our prior impressions of the whole picture. The problem arises when the prior understanding with which we approach the individual passages is influenced more by external presuppositions than by previous readings of the biblical material. The key factor in the overall picture which seems to have had the greatest influence on interpretation is the concept of headship which is seen in terms of authority and submission. Therefore in an attempt to come to terms with this problem in the writings of Paul, after considering the relationship of women to God, we will take a bird's eye view of the area of headship – authority – submission before coming to a detailed treatment of the passages where Paul deals with the marriage relationship and with the position of women within the church.[2]

1. PAUL : WOMAN IN RELATION TO GOD

'In Christ Jesus you are all sons of God, through faith. For as many of you as were baptized into Christ have put on Christ. There is neither Jew nor Greek, there is neither slave nor free, there is neither male nor female; for you are all one in Christ Jesus. And if you are Christ's then you are Abraham's offspring, heirs according to promise' (Galatians 3:26–29).

These verses make explicit what is clear throughout the whole of the New Testament, that in relation to God, men and women stand in exactly the same position. Kümmel summarises the New Testament view of man: 'Man is seen solely as the one who stands before God. He is created by God and is in duty bound in obedience to his creator. He tries to set himself up against God and thus becomes a sinner in the sight of God. His sin does not have root in his natural bodily existence. Rather, Man is essentially a unity, whose whole being stands over against God and is therefore ripe for His final judgment.'[3] This is true of both females and males. Both are sinners standing in need of salvation. Similarly both are eligible for salvation through faith in Jesus Christ.

In Christ, both male and female have common access to the Father in prayer, share in the indwelling of the Holy Spirit and in the priesthood of all believers (Ephesians 5:18–20; Philippians 4:6–7, etc. Cf 1 Peter 2:4–10). Don Cupitt points out that in spite of the fact that the view of the church through the ages concerning the male-female relation had been strongly and adversely influenced by a non-biblical world view, nevertheless, 'Christianity from the first held as a matter of theological principle that women are equally capable of salvation, have equal access to public worship and may live in a state of religious dedication.'[4]

The fact that most books dealing with the doctrine of Man in the New Testament never discuss what relation sexuality has to Man's relationship to God[5] is an indication of how clearly the New Testament presents the equality of the sexes before God. There is a tendency for some scholars[6] to include a discussion on women merely as one topic in a section on how a man should live his Christian life, but this is not general nor is it the approach of the New Testament. There women, like men, stand before God primarily as human beings.

In a patriarchal society, 'social and cosmic reality is defined according to the way in which the male members of the society perceive reality.'[7] That is, male members of the society define both male and female roles and values; the male way of understanding reality is then internalized by all. The society becomes man's society where women are allowed a place. That this picture has sometimes been true of the Church in history is clear, as for example, where 'protestant emphasis on the universal priesthood of believers seems to have meant male believers; since the priesthood of women was envisaged almost solely in terms of motherhood and childbearing.'[8] However, this is not true of the church envisaged by Paul. The body of Christ consists of males and females. Women not only belong to the church, they are the church, just as the men are.

While all acknowledge the equal status and equal worth of male and female in the sight of God, there has been much debate concerning the precise meaning and implications of Galatians 3:28. Some have assumed that it implies the removal of all role distinctions within the church,[9] others that it merely means that all have equal access to the church through baptism, but does not alter the distinctive roles of Jew and Greek, bond and free, or male and female.[10] Caird points out that the three pairs must be seen in parallel. We cannot press the first two into saying that male/female distinctions disappear – particularly as the form of words used for the third pair is slightly different from that used for the first two apparently in order to avoid this implication.[11] However, it would be wrong so to spiritualize the third pair that we end up by saying that 'Paul's long running battle with the Judaizers, his determined struggle to maintain visible unity... need never have happened.'[12] We cannot limit the meaning of the phrase 'there is no male and female' to denote simply that both are permitted to be baptized unless we put the same limitations on the first two pairs which would somewhat lessen the force of Paul's words. Paul seems to be saying that all these divisions 'can have no place in the thought or practice of those who are united with Christ.'[13]

It is right to emphasise that Paul here 'is more interested in the unity rather than the equality that the Gospel brings'.[14] It is a unity which has practical consequences for the relation between Jew and Greek, between slave and free and between male and female, but the primary concern here is the relation of each to God. It is clear that females relate to God in exactly the same way as males. The use of the word 'sons' in verse 26 for both males and females brings this home. All Christians, whether slave or free, whether male or female, are 'sons of God'. As sons, enjoying full liberties and privileges, they become heirs who are entitled to all that the Father's resources can give them.[15] These verses, then, prohibit any interpretation of such verses as 1 Corinthians 11:3 or 7 which would imply any difference in the relation of the sexes to God.

2. PAUL : WOMAN IN RELATION TO MAN (I)

Introduction

There is much in Paul's epistles about the relationships between Christians. He talks of their unity, their mutual responsibility, mutual love and mutual submission.[16] However, apart from passages where he is dealing specifically with the husband-wife relation, Paul in fact has very little to say about the relation between men and women as such. Ryder Smith points out[17] that 'just as most of the New Testament references to men are made to them not as men but as persons, so most of its references to women are made to them not as women but as persons.' When we consider the verses where Paul does deal with the male-female relation, it must always be kept in mind that he saw the primary relation between Christian men and Christian women as their unity in Christ. Galatians 3:28 remains the most explicit reference to the male-female relation found anywhere in Paul's letters.

There are twelve occasions on which Paul refers in any way to the relationship between men and women as such. Of these, six refer specifically and clearly to the marriage relation (Romans 7:2; 1 Corinthians 7; Ephesians 5:21–33; Colossians 3:18–19; 1 Thessalonians 4:4; and Titus 2:4–5). Three (1 Corinthians 11:3–16; 14:34–35; 1 Timothy 2:8–15) are in the context of behaviour at gatherings of the church; where it is not absolutely clear if the reference is to men and women in general or to husbands and wives. Of the remaining three, Galatians 3:28, we have already discussed; 1 Timothy 5:2–3 tells Timothy to treat 'older women like mothers, younger women like sisters in all purity' and to 'honour widows who are real widows'; and Romans 1:26–27 talks of 'natural relations' between people of different sexes and 'unnatural relations' between people of the same sex. The primary reference of this latter is of course to physical relations, but it does bring home the fact that Paul in Galatians 3:28 does not in any way mean to obscure the difference between maleness and femaleness in Man.

Before we look in detail at what Paul is saying in these first nine passages, let us, because of their influence on interpretation, consider briefly the concepts of headship, authority and submission.

Headship, Authority and Submission

Scripture teaches quite clearly that the husband is the head of the wife (Ephesians 5:23) and possibly that the head of the woman is the man (1 Corinthians 11:3) although this could also be seen as referring to husband and wife. It is generally assumed that the meaning of headship is self-evident, as Fisher, 'The particular emphasis is that of superiority and rulership ';[18] or Grosheide, 'Of every man it can be said that he is above the woman'[19]; or Ladd, 'Paul retains the Jewish idea of the subordination of woman to man.'[20] Thus it is taken for granted that headship means having authority over, or being the boss. The Good News Bible builds this assumption into its translation, so we have in 1 Corinthians 11:3, 'the husband is supreme over the wife' and in Ephesians 5:23, '...has authority over...'.

However, it is important to remember that 'head' used in this context is a metaphor and there is no reason to suppose that the first century use of this metaphor will be identical with its twentieth century use, particularly as in the first century it was the heart not the head that was seen as the source of thought and reason, the head at this time being seen rather as the source of life. Thus, if we are to use the principle of headship as the key to the way we ought to understand the whole relationship between the sexes, it is very important that we make sure we understand the principle itself correctly. Let us consider then, firstly, the background to the term and, secondly, the way in which Paul uses it. The idea of a husband being the head of a wife was not prevalent at the time. The metaphor used in this way appears to be original to Paul[21], therefore we must look to Paul to supply its meaning rather than to the contemporary view of male-female relations.

a) In Greek, *kephale* ('head') is not used in the sense of ruler or chief but it is sometimes used in the sense of source or origin – as the source or head of a river. However, in Hebrew the word *rosh* ('head') can be used in a metaphorical sense as 'chief over' although even here the idea is often of priority rather than of controlling influence, or authority as such.[22] It is clear that Paul, as a Hebrew speaker, could quite definitely have had the idea of head meaning 'chief over' in mind and thus have envisaged a relationship of authority and submission. But it is equally apparent that writing in Greek for Greek speaking readers he would have to make it quite clear in the text that this was his intention, as otherwise it would not have been understood in this way. Let us then consider the two occasions where Paul uses the term to describe the relationship between man and woman, not at this stage to provide a detailed exegesis, but to discover whether the context can most easily support the interpretation of headship as concerned with source or origin, or whether it is necessary to introduce the concept of authority in order to understand the passage.

b) 1 Corinthians 11:3 is the first passage to consider. Is there anything in the context to show that we should interpret headship here as indicating an authority/submission relation? The word submission does not, in fact, occur in the passage and although the word for authority does occur, it refers to the authority of the woman herself and not the authority of the man over the woman.[23]

It is sometimes assumed that Paul's references to the Creation narratives should themselves be seen as indicating the subjection of the woman, but even if one were to accept that this concept was clearly presented in Genesis, it seems much more likely that the Greek speaking readers would see the mention of woman being created from man as emphasising the idea of origin rather than as introducing the idea of authority.

Similarly in verse 3 itself, Christ is spoken of as being the head of every man, and Christ does, without any doubt, have authority, therefore it is suggested that authority must be the basic meaning of headship. However, it is equally true that Christ is the source of all things and in Colossians 1:18 Christ is spoken of as 'the head' of the church in the context of his being before all things and the source of creation. The idea of source also makes sense in the phrase, 'the head of Christ is God', and incidentally removes some of the problems of subordinationism in the Godhead that have arisen from this verse.[24] Chrysostom, who himself regarded women as very much in subjection to men, nevertheless takes the Christological context in verse 3 to mean that subjection could not be the point at issue here, 'For had Paul meant to speak of rule and subjection as thou sayest, he would not have brought forward the instance of a wife, but rather of a slave and master.'[25] He thought that the point of the verse was rather the union between the head and the body, though he also saw the idea of origin being present. We should 'accept the notion of a perfect union and the first principle,' although Chrysostom too warns against pressing the analogy too far. 'For both the union is surer and the beginning more honourable in the Godhead.'[26]

Thus one cannot automatically assume that the context of 1 Corinthians 11:3 supports the use of the term 'head' as implying a relation of authority/submission between men and women. It is interesting to note that earlier in this same epistle Paul had used the term authority in connection with the husband/wife relationship in a case where the husband does have authority over his wife, but where this authority is exactly paralleled by the authority of the wife over her husband (1 Corinthians 7:4).[27]

c) In Ephesians 5:21–23 the headship of the husband is found alongside the concept of the submission of the wife and could therefore imply a position of authority.[28] However, two points must be noted. Firstly, though the passage does provide the analogy of the headship of Christ over the church, this headship is not interpreted in terms of the authority which Christ undoubtedly has, but rather in terms of his loving and giving of himself on behalf of the church; it seems logical therefore that the headship of the husband should also be interpreted in this way.

Secondly, rather than seeing the subjection of the wife as a direct consequence of the headship of the husband over her, the passage presents a conflict between the two ideas. Although most translators obscure the fact,[29] verse 24 begins with a strong 'but' (*alla*), so we have, 'the husband is the head of the wife. . . . But as the church is subject to Christ, so let wives also be subject.' If we assume that headship means authority, then the 'but' is difficult and a 'therefore' would make more sense. If, however, we follow the analogy provided by Paul and see the headship of the husband as indicating that he should love his wife and give himself fully on her behalf, then the 'but' makes good sense and we can leave the text as it stands. The husband is to love and serve his wife, yes – but she *also* is to be subject to him. Thus the passage can be seen as forming a natural development in the husband/wife context of the call to mutual submission within the church that Paul gives in verse 21.

d) It may be helpful at this stage to note here some points regarding the meaning of the word used for submission or subjection (*hupotasso*). The root meaning of the word is 'to order', 'to arrange' or 'to put in place'.[30] In Pauline writings it occurs twenty-three times as a verb and eight times in various noun forms. Paul appears to make a clear distinction between submission, as that required from a wife to her husband, and obedience, as required from a child to his parents or from a slave to his master. He never uses the word for obedience in a husband/wife context.[31]

As far as humans are concerned, submission is always voluntary. Only God is ever seen as subjecting others, whether he subjects them to himself, to another, or to futility (e.g. 1 Corinthians 15:24–28; Romans 8:20; Philippians 3:21; Ephesians 1:21–22). 'In all these cases the act of subjugation and the fate of those who submit reveal the existence of a hierarchy. . . . The weaker is "put into its place".'[32] However, within the New Testament, no ruler or authority of any kind, within or without the church, is ever told to subject others to or to take any action to ensure the submission of others. (This does not mean that authority is never given, but that the word for submission, which is used to describe the relationship between Christians and in particular between wife and husband, would not be appropriate in that context.) Rather in all cases where humans are involved Paul describes 'a voluntary attitude of giving in, co-operating, assuming responsibility and carrying a burden. He expects this kind of subordination only of Christ and of persons who are in Christ.'[33] The word can be used for the ordering of a military column and perhaps the emphasis here should be on the wife 'ordering herself under' her husband rather than on submission as such. As Karl Barth puts it,[34] 'Of course the word does speak of subordination but in such a way that the emphasis is on mutual adaptation and co-ordination. The authority to which the woman bows in her subordination to man is not the latter's but that of the *taxis* (order) to which both are subject.' Thus the subjection to which the wife is called is a voluntary putting first of the will and desires of the husband, seeking his benefit. Ephesians 5:21 shows us that submission does not have to be a one-way thing, it can be mutual.

e) It should be pointed out here that in 1 Timothy 2:12 Paul does tell us that he permits no woman to teach or have authority over a man (or again, possibly, no wife over her husband). This passage will be discussed more fully at a later stage, but two points should be noted in this context. Firstly, the verb used in 1 Timothy 2:12 for 'to have authority' is not the verb formed from the normal word for authority (*exousia*), but a little used verb (*authentein*), a strong word with a sense of self-directed domineering. The KJV catches something of the idea with 'to usurp authority'. Thus it is possible that Paul is here referring to a particular kind of authority which the woman does not have and is not to use. Secondly, it is not made explicit that the reverse of Paul's statement should apply. That is, it is not self-evident that Paul in stating that the woman is not to usurp authority over the man is implying that the man has authority over the woman. The implication may be there but the case would need to be argued.

In making all of these points it is not being argued that there is no difference in the way that men and women relate to each other. However, what we have tried to show is that as we approach the New Testament passages it would be wrong to do so with the prior assumption that the overall biblical view[35] is that the relationship between man and woman and in particular between husband and wife is primarily to be considered in terms of the one having authority over the other. It may be that other presuppositions are equally inapplicable; we have considered this particular one simply because it occurs so frequently.

3. PAUL : WOMAN IN RELATION TO HER HUSBAND

Paul saw marriage as a primary, binding and exclusive relation; exclusive even within the close-knit Christian community. He stressed the permanent nature of the bond, as in Romans 7:2 where, when Paul says 'a married woman is bound by law to her husband as long as he lives', there is the implicit assumption that this is how it ought to be. This permanency of the marriage bond is made explicit in 1 Corinthians 7. Paul stressed also the dignity and value of marriage for its own sake as part of God's plan and as the truest illustration of the love between Christ and the church. The importance of the Christian home as a foundation for Christian living is similarly brought out strongly in Paul's writings. It is interesting that the description in Ephesians 6 of the Christian soldier and the armour that he needs to withstand 'the wiles of the devil', follows on directly from the description of relationships within the Christian home.

Before coming to any conclusions concerning Paul's view of the nature of the relationship between a wife and her husband, let us consider particular passages in detail.

1 Corinthians 7

This chapter is a turning point within the first letter to the Corinthians. Here, Paul begins to answer various specific questions raised by the Corinthians in a letter which they had sent to him. However, the chapter must also be seen in context and any view that chapter 7 contains a negative opinion of the body, seeing it as something to be despised, is certainly ruled out of court by 1 Corinthians 6:19 – 'Do you not know that your body is a temple of the Holy Spirit within you?'

It is clear that in answering their questions, Paul sometimes quotes from their letter; from the way he does this it is apparent that they had not simply asked questions, but in their letter 'they had put their own case and expected Paul to agree with them.'[36] There appears to have been a strict party who saw sexual asceticism as mandatory[37] and who were possibly even considering renouncing their own marriages.[38] Paul replies, giving advice to the married, to those married to unbelievers, to the unmarried, to the betrothed, and to the widowed, as to what their behaviour in these times should be. He agrees that he does prefer the celibate state, but only in the context of the 'impending distress'. Marriage is by no means to be seen as an abberation, rather it is the norm, and Paul 'roundly condemns'[39] any ascetical tendencies within marriage.

The key to Paul's thinking in this chapter appears to be his eschatological perspective. He seems to expect the second coming to take place very soon and there is a sense of urgency at the shortness of the time; nevertheless his advice also contains a built-in warning against any 'over-realization' of eschatology which would give no thought to the way life should be lived in the meanwhile. It is interesting that as in Galatians 3:28, the Jew/ Greek (vv 17–20) and slave/free (vv 21–24) relations are brought up and discussed here alongside the male/female relation. At Corinth, the whole society was based on certain racial, sexual and social values and that particular society would not have been able to exist without those values. Paul's preaching in many ways negated these values and he seeks here to deal with some of the resulting socio-logical problems.[40]

This chapter is not and does not set out to be a systematic treatment of sex or of the theology of marriage, but it does give some insight into Paul's thought concerning this area. Probably the most striking and significant feature of the chapter is its structure, where Paul from beginning to end treats men and women as equals, addressing them both in turn with an almost exact parallelism. This is the more striking when one realizes that almost all of the moral treatises of the time were addressed solely to men and even where women are brought in, we never find anything approaching the complete impartiality which Paul shows here. Both men and women are treated as having equal worth and as being 'equally educable in the field of moral responsibility'.[41] The woman is not approached from a wholly different angle, rather there is reciprocity in every way. There is no impression given that all the decisions are made by the men with the women simply making the appropriate response. When we consider that in the Christian society generally, as in the world as a whole, this is probably what happened, Paul's approach is very surprising.

Keeping in mind this reciprocity and also the fact that the whole chapter is written in the context of the last time, let us consider what Paul's advice given here has to tell us about his attitude to male-female relationships and to the place of women.

1 Cor. 7:1–7 These verses deal with marriage and the exercise of conjugal rights within marriage. The strength of any argument which sees an ascetic tendency within Paul, or even a preference for celibacy as such, depends to some extent on whether v 1b, 'it is well for a man not to touch a woman', is taken as a quote from the Corinthians' letter or as Paul's own opinion.[42] However, in either case, v 2, 'each man should have his own wife and each woman her own husband', makes it clear that marriage is the rule, although both marriage and celibacy are to be seen as gifts.

The discussion of conjugal rights in verses 3 and 4 shows that Paul has no time at all for any idealization of virginity. In marriage, sex relations are not a might but a must. The idea of a wife having any 'conjugal rights' at all would be startling enough in a society where the passive role of the wife was continually emphasized, but Paul goes on to say that the authority which the husband has over the wife in this respect, is exactly paralleled by her authority over him. This is the only occasion in the New Testament where the word *exousiazo* (to have power or authority over) is particularly applied to the relation between husband and wife,[43] and in this instance the authority is mutual.

These verses do 'indicate that whatever Paul may have to say elsewhere about the submission of wives to their husbands, this was no absolute affair.'[44]

1 Cor. 7:8–11 The recommendation to the unmarried and widowed to remain single, and the insistence that those who are married should remain so, are again addressed equally to men and women. These verses show that whatever Paul's preference for celibacy (and 1 Timothy 5:14, 'I would have the younger widows marry' must be taken into account in any overall assessment), he is by no means implying that marriage is intrinsically and in all circumstances less perfect than singleness. A marriage is not to be entered into lightly, but once in existence it is a permanent bond and there is no question of a married believer deciding to set aside his or her marriage.

1 Cor. 7:12–24   In the case of an already existing marriage where one partner is an unbeliever, Paul does permit divorce, but only if initiated by the unbelieving partner, whether male or female. That such a marriage is far from ideal is shown by 2 Corinthians 6:14–18 where Paul speaks out against the formation of any partnership of this kind between believer and unbeliever. Nevertheless it remains a marriage and is therefore not to be lightly set aside. Like Jesus (Mark 10:12), and unlike the Jewish law, Paul assumes that both partners have equal rights relating to divorce, and an equal responsibility to avoid it.[45]

1 Cor. 7:25–38   J. K. Eliot argues that the whole of this section is written to those who are betrothed, therefore he translates verse 27 as 'Are you engaged to a woman? Do not seek to be free', and verse 29 as, 'Let those who are engaged live as though they were not.'[46] This involves translating *gunē* as 'woman' rather than as 'wife' throughout these verses. If this is done then any possible contradiction with Paul's advice in verses 3 and 4 is avoided. Whether Eliot is correct or not, it is clear that Paul's advice to those considering marriage is that they should remain unmarried; not because marriage is in any sense wrong, but rather because he would spare them anxiety. As Bruce puts it, 'The conflict of interests and cares to which Christians with family responsibilities are ordinarily subject is intensified in times of "distress" and Paul wants his readers to be free from such worries.'[47] There is no disdain of marriage as such, but in the last times, to be married is harder than to be single and Paul has a pastoral concern here both for the individuals concerned and for the church as a whole.

Not only is it easier to be unmarried, but the unmarried also have more time and energy to give to service. In verse 34, 'the unmarried woman or girl is anxious about the affairs of the Lord', Paul shows clearly that he has no time for those who would suggest that the only, or even the proper, vocation for a woman is to be found in marriage and motherhood. The exact parallel between male and female must again be noted. For the married, whether male or female, there is a natural tendency to spend time in building relationships. Héring sees verses 33 and 34b ('is anxious ...how to please his/her wife/husband'), not as condeming such behaviour, that is, as suggesting that they seek to please their partners when they really ought to be concentrating on Christian service, nor even as simply stating a fact, but rather as laying down the norm for behaviour appropriate to the married.[48] Thus Paul is showing how seriously he takes the primary responsibilities of married people towards their families. It is interesting to note that

1 Corinthians 7 supports the concept of the place of the wife being in the home just to the extent that it supports the concept of the place of the husband being in the home.

Conzelmann believes that in verse 34 where Paul speaks of the concern of the unmarried girl to be 'holy in body', the 'ascetic tendency is plain' although he would agree that as elsewhere 'it is not elevated into a principle'.[49] However, Paul is not here elevating virginity nor is he suggesting that the unmarried as such, are more righteous than the married but rather he points out that their consecration is unmodified by any earthly commitment.'[50] 'How to be holy in body and spirit' does not suggest any element of moral superiority, but rather clarifies the way in which the unmarried women seek to please the Lord.

From this chapter it is possible to identify four principles which appear to be governing Paul's thought.
- a. In view of the fact that 'the appointed time has grown very short', Paul would recommend celibacy to the Corinthians.
- b. In spite of the urgency of the times, marriage, once entered into, is not something to be set aside, or even to be considered of less value than celibacy.
- c. There is between men and women what Kahler calls a 'gleichwertigen Gegenseitigheit',[51] a reciprocity of equal worth, shown especially in marriage.
- d. Marriage and celibacy are both to be seen as 'gifts' to be used in the service of God, so that, 'in whatever state each was called, there let him remain with God' (v 24).

Ephesians 5:21–33[52]

Like 1 Corinthians 7, this passage is not intended to be a comprehensive setting out of every aspect of the marriage relation, and should not be treated as such. Whereas in 1 Corinthians 7 the directing motive was eschatology and the urgency of the times, here it is the incomprehensible reality of the love of Christ for his church.[53] There has been some debate as to whether the husband/wife theme or the Christ/Church theme is the dominant idea of the passage, and whether or not one is simply an illustration to explain or expand the meaning of the other. However, as Markus Barth points out, 'A decision between them need not be made... both topics are central and both are, ontologically and noetically, so closely tied together that they cannot be unstrung.'[54] Some would suggest that in this section Paul is using, imitating or adapting a previously known pagan *Haustafel* (code of rules relating to the running of a household), but this is debatable.[55] If he is, then Paul, by introducing new ideas and by linking so closely the relation between husband and wife and that between Christ and church, certainly transforms the form and makes it his own.

Eph. 5:21–22 'Be subject to one another out of reverence for Christ. Wives (be subject) to your husbands as to the Lord.' The fact that the verb is left out of verse 22, linking the two verses together by making the second dependent on the verb from the first, indicates that the 'deference which wives are to show to their husbands is a particular aspect of that submission which all Christians have been urged to show to one another.'[56] Verse 21 makes it clear that for Paul the idea of mutual submission was not a contradiction in terms and warns us to beware of interpreting the relationship in hierarchical terms. It should be noted that this subjection which is called for from all Christians and in particular from wives to their husbands involves a deliberate decision to give priority to the other person.[57]

Eph. 5:23 'For the husband is head of the wife as Christ is head of the church his body, and is himself its Saviour.' In this verse, the addition of the phrase, 'and is himself its Saviour' makes two things clear. Firstly that Paul is seeing the headship of Christ over the Church in terms of his total self-giving for them, his salvation of them, rather than in terms of his rule and authority. 'As Christ is the deliverer and defender of the church, . . . so (the implication seems to be) the husband is the protector of his wife.'[58] It is possible, as M. Barth does, to see the parallel with Christ's headship of the church as in fact limiting the extent of the headship that a man has over his wife. In Ephesians 1:22–23 we have a description of Christ as head over all things, the emphasis here being quite clearly on his rule. However, he is the head of the church, as Ephesians 4:15–16 explains, in a distinct and different fashion. He enables her to grow, knits her into a unity, and nourishes her. A man is said in Ephesians 5 to be head of his wife not in the way that Christ is sovereign of all (including the church) but in the particular way that Christ is head of the church. 'In short, a headship qualified, interpreted and limited by Christ alone is proclaimed, not an unlimited headship that can be arbitrarily defined and has to be endured.'[59]

Secondly, the descriptions of Christ as Saviour of the church shows that there are certain aspects of Christ's relation to his church that can never be paralleled in the relation between man and wife. A man may imitate Christ's self-giving love but in no sense can he be the 'Saviour' of his wife. Perhaps Kähler[60] is right to see the husband/wife relation as a 'Leitbild', or example, rather than as an 'Abbild', or copy, of the Christ/Church relation. J. Hurley assumes that verse 23 'presents the model of Christ's headship as the reason for a wife's submission' and thus concludes that the authority/submission concept must be included in the husband's headship of the wife, but this again completely ignores the 'but' with which verse 24 begins.[61]

Eph. 5:24 'But as the church is subject to Christ, so let wives be subject in everything to their husbands.' Most translators, seeing subjection largely in terms of obedience, and headship largely in terms of rule, have had difficulty with the *alla* or 'but' that introduces this verse. The RSV omits it altogether and leaves the impression that it would like to follow the KJV in replacing the 'but' with a 'therefore', completely negating the adversative sense. The NIV and the TEV also omit the 'but'. The NEB does include it by saying that even though Christ – unlike the husband – is the Saviour of the church, nevertheless the wife is still to be subject to her husband. However, the verse as it stands, including the 'but', seems to make more sense if we take it as meaning that even though the husband as 'head' of the wife is to serve her and give himself fully on her behalf, nevertheless the wife must not think that that places her in a special position without responsibilities, for just as the church is subject to Christ, she too is to be subject to her husband in everything.

Eph. 5:25–30 That it is the self-giving aspect of Christ's relation with his church that is paralleled in the relation of man and wife is confirmed in verse 25, 'Husbands love your wives as Christ loved the church and gave himself up for her.'

It is possible to see this verse as contrasting with verse 23 (although in this instance there is no 'but' to indicate a contrast!), that is, as saying that even though he is her head, the husband must not take advantage but must love his wife. However, it seems better to see the whole passage as a unity, with verses 25ff elucidating the meaning of headship in verse 23 rather than contrasting with it, and also with the imperative 'love' of verse 25 bringing out the meaning to husband of the 'be subject' of verse 21.

Paul here becomes taken up by the tremendous nature of the love of Christ for the church and at times the parallel relation becomes lost. The husband can never be seen as a duplicate of Christ. This is made quite clear by the way in which Paul speaks of Christ. Nevertheless the love of Christ is the source of and example for the husband's love of his wife. Bruce makes this point when he says of verse 28, where husbands are exhorted to 'love their wives as their own bodies', 'Paul does not overdo the analogy and speak of the wife as her husband's body, as the church is Christ's body.'[62] Rather Paul refers to the one 'one flesh' concept of Genesis 2:24. We must take note of the fact that, although in this chapter parallels with marriage are raised, neither here nor elsewhere in the New Testament is Christ described as the husband of the church, but only as the bridegroom with the church as the bride. Maybe this is another warning lest we press the analogy too far.

It has sometimes been assumed that this passage teaches that the wife is to submit not to her husband's authority, but to his love,[63] or even that 'where there is no love Paul does not expect submission.'[64] However, nowhere in the chapter is there any indication that this is so. Both the submission of the wife and the love of the husband are grounded in their relationship to Christ and are not dependent on whether or not the spouse fulfils his or her obligations.

Eph. 5:31–33 After quoting Genesis 2:24, Paul in verse 32 says, 'This is a great mystery and I take it to mean Christ and the Church.' It is not quite clear what it is that Paul is describing as a mystery. 'This' could refer to the relation between Christ and the church, to 'human marriage at its best',[65] to neither of these relations, but rather to the relation of both relationships to one another,[66] or to verse 31 itself with 'mystery' being used in the sense of allegory, which is then explained by verse 32. Whichever explanation applies, Paul shows that he is concerned also with the literal sense of Genesis 2:24, and he returns to the practical lesson in verse 33: 'However, let each one of you love his wife as himself, and let the wife see that she respects her husband.'

This passage as a whole indicates then that both the subjection of the wife and the love of the husband are in fact to be expressions in different ways of the mutual subjection called for in verse 21. Both can be seen in terms of a readiness to subordinate one's own will and advantage for the benefit of the other. Paul describes 'the union between husband and wife as a give and take, an exchange of offering and receiving, seeking and finding, tension and fulfilment'.[67] He gives us a picture of marriage that has rarely, if ever, been surpassed. That he can use marriage as an illustration to symbolize the relationship between Christ and the church reflects the tremendously high value that is placed on marriage and is a further indication of the fact that passages like 1 Corinthians 7 are not to be seen as in any sense a depreciation of marriage.

However, it must be pointed out that, while it is true that these exhortations, to the wife to be subject and to the husband to love, do not take away the responsibility of the wife to love her husband or of the husband to be subject to his wife, nevertheless Paul's deliberate choice of different terms and in fact his use of the parallel relationship show that he was very much aware that just as the roles of Christ and the church are not interchangeable, so neither are the roles of husband and wife.

Colossians 3:18–19

'Wives be subject to your husbands as is fitting in the Lord. Husbands love your wives and do not be harsh with them.'

In these, as in the following verses, Paul is dealing more with the practical outworkings of relationships than with their theological bases.

Col. 3:18 Some commentators take it for granted that the 'be subject' here is equivalent to 'obey',[68] but it appears that Paul had carefully chosen the term in contrast to the 'children obey' of verse 20 and the 'slaves obey' of verse 22. Nowhere in the New Testament is a wife exhorted to obey her husband and we have shown that the concept of obedience is by no means the main emphasis of the word for subjection (*hupotassesthe*).[69] It is possible that the 'as is fitting in the Lord' is meant not so much as a justification, a reason why wives should be subject, but rather as an explanation and as a limitation of the way in which that subjection should be applied. As Martin expresses it, one should 'act and respond to others in a ... way which expresses a type of life suitable to those who belong to Christ.'[70] There is no detailed instruction given here or for that matter elsewhere in Paul's writings as to exactly what is or is not fitting in this context. Lohse suggests that this will be determined by custom and tradition.[71]

Col. 3:19 As in Ephesians 5 the husband is exhorted to love (*agapate*) his wife. 'This is not only a matter of affectionate feeling or sexual attraction; it involves his active and unceasing care for her well-being.'[72] The addition of 'do not be harsh with them' was maybe felt by Paul to be specifically necessary because of some situation at Colossae which remains unknown to us. It can hardly be seen as an explanatory comment on the nature of *agape* love.

It is significant that in his comments here, Paul addresses both husbands and wives. This in itself as Moule points out was 'an outstanding Christian innovation, as contrasted with the pagan examples (i.e. of *Haustafeln*) – the stress upon the reciprocal nature of the duties'.[73] Again we have the implication that there is order in the relationship between husband and wife, but very little indication as to the meaning or significance or consequences of that order.

1 Thessalonians 4:3–6

In these verses Paul again stresses the value to be placed on
marriage and the fact that the marriage relation is sacred in the
sight of God. In verses 3–5, 'This is the will of God... that each
one of you know how to take a wife for himself in holiness and
honour, not in the passion of lust like heathen who do not know
God', Paul is not denigrating the sexual aspects of marriage.
Immorality is seen as a bar to sanctification, but marriage most
certainly is not. Rather Paul is pointing out that marriage is much
more than merely a means for gratifying sexual desire, and unlike
the practice of the heathen, a wife is not to be regarded simply as a
sex object. As Stendahl puts it, 'Woman must not be regarded as a
sexual being, but as destined to eternal life.'[74]

Although it is not spelt out, the implication seems to be that
there had been problems of adultery in the Thessalonian church.
Paul therefore re-emphasizes the sanctity of marriage as ordained
by God so that 'whoever disregards this, disregards not man but
God' (verse 8).

1 Timothy 5:14

'So I would have younger widows marry, bear children, rule
their households and give the enemy no occasion to revile us.'

This verse does not refer directly to the relation between husband
and wife, but it does have some bearing on that relation. In order to
avoid the temptations to violate their pledge or to indulge in
idleness and gossip, rather than joining the official list of widows,
younger widows are advised to re-marry, have some children and
'rule their households'. A major motivation for the advice given
here is again the apostle's anxiety 'that unnecessary reproach from
any non-Christian opponent should be avoided.'[75]

Thus, again we have emphasis placed on the value of marriage.
'The wife and mother holds an office at least as honourable and
fruitful as that of the enrolled pensioner and servant of the
church.'[76] As Dibelius and Conzelmann put it, 'The ideal of
Christian citizenship of the Pastorals is shown in an ordinance
based upon the founding of families.'[77] However, it is unnecessary
to see, as they do, a conflict between the teaching here and that of
Paul in 1 Corinthians 7, for here we are dealing specifically with the
re-marriage of younger widows whereas there the teaching is more
general and eschatological considerations were paramount. Kelly
may be right in his suggestion that Paul saw the ideal as being for

anyone, whether male or female, to avoid a second marriage, 'but his good sense and realism made him encourage second marriages where the strain involved in remaining single would be too great.'[78] This passage then ties in with the teaching of 1 Corinthians 7:36–38.

It is significant that the verb to rule (*oikodespoteō*) is used to describe a wife's function in the home. This verb occurs only here in the New Testament, but the noun *oikodespotes* occurs twelve times and 'it denotes the "master of the house" who has control over the *oikos* (household) in the widest sense.'[79] Although the husband is part of the household and is not specifically excluded from the rule of the wives that is mentioned here, it does seem likely that 'when wives "rule their households" they are not giving up their submissiveness, but are acting as the female counterpart of their husband, the householder.'[80] Nevertheless the use of such a strong word does seem to show that Paul saw the husband and the wife as standing together in their management of the household and indicates clearly that decision making and ruling were by no means the sole prerogative of the husband.

Titus 2:1–6

We have here practical instructions for the behaviour of men and women. The younger women are to be taught by the older women to 'love their husbands and children, to be sensible, chaste, domestic, kind and submissive to their husbands' (v 4). They must understand that their family lives are an important area of Christian witness. The motive for their behaviour is again that the word of God should not be discredited or blasphemed. In this context perhaps this would suggest that Paul is thinking particularly of their non-Christian husbands but this is speculation and the concern could just as easily be for their neighbours. Leaney sees Paul's concern as a confirmation that 'the church is anxious that the relative freedom of a Christian woman should not give to the world an impression of licence.'[81] The over-riding concern throughout the whole chapter is that all Christians should behave in such a way that their calling could never be spoken against and 'so that in everything they may adorn the doctrine of God our Saviour' (2:10).

Woman in Relation to her Husband : Conclusion

The only other passages which could possibly be seen as being relevant to the husband/wife relationship are those which deal primarily with behaviour in worship and we will discuss them fully under that heading. From the passages we have considered, we learn much of Paul's attitude to marriage, but it is important to note that Paul's instructions and advice are all of a general nature. Nowhere does he speak of a perfect 'marriage order', or an 'ideal marriage pattern'. He provides very clear guidelines, but 'there is no obligation to a fixed model that can be copied throughout all generations.'[82]

Paul's own experience, as well as his teaching in 1 Corinthians 7 makes it clear that marriage is not the only option for the Christian, but nevertheless Paul did see it as a vitally important part of God's plan, reflecting even the relationship between Christ and his church. He taught that '*i*. Marriage is an indissoluble covenant enduring throughout life; *ii*. It is an exclusive fellowship between two persons; *iii*. The spouses enter into an obligation to each other in respect of all they are and possess.'[83] Paul presents us with a picture of marriage that is amazingly egalitarian, particularly in the light of the conditions of the time. He advocated neither a patriarchal nor a matriarchal structure. It is often suggested that the use of such terms as 'head' and 'submission' is evidence that Paul did see a hierarchical order in marriage, but we have shown that these terms are not necessarily used in that way. Rather Paul emphasises the total responsibility of each partner towards the other.

Paul is equally concerned about the responsibilities of husband and of wife in the marriage and in the home. For example, in 1 Timothy 3:4,12, elders and deacons are required to manage or rule their households well, and in 1 Timothy 3:14 the younger widows are urged to marry and rule their households. It may be that 'household' in the first instance includes the wife and in the second instance excludes the husband, but the text itself gives us no real reason to come to that conclusion. The common ascription to the husband of the title 'head of the household' is never found in Scripture and verses like 1 Timothy 3:14 would seem to indicate that it is perhaps a less appropriate title than some have supposed. Similarly, no support can be found in the Pauline writings for the view that the home is an incidental part of a man's life but the total purpose of a woman's. Rather it is an essential basis within, but not the totality of, the life of both. Both are called upon to fulfil their responsibilities within the home, and 1 Corinthians 7:33–34 shows that Paul saw this as a priority for Christians who are married, but both are called upon also to fulfil their responsibilities within the wider fellowship of the church and even towards the world outside. Service and love of God were to be the supreme motive in the life of both.

There is a very positive attitude towards sex in marriage. Ephesians 5 in particular shows that Paul did not see procreation as the only or even as the primary purpose of marriage, but rather the expression of mutual self-giving love in all its aspects.

There are indications that Paul did see the husband as in some way prior to the relationship, as first in the order within marriage. However, he nowhere expands on this priority and we are not entitled to presuppose that it involved authority. It may mean that the husband, like the first-born, acts as the representative and the spokesman, but this can be only speculation. Perhaps the way in which this is applied will vary from couple to couple.

It is clear that Paul was concerned that the institution of marriage be held in respect and that the behaviour of Christians should never be such as to lead outsiders to think that they held marriage in low esteem. Paul introduced principles relating to marriage which would inevitably lead to a change in the attitudes and the patterns of behaviour common at the time, but he never directly calls for such changes. The Christians were to be aware of the attitudes, ideals and laws of their society and to behave in such a way as was 'fitting in the Lord', and as brought honour to his name.

4. PAUL : WOMAN IN RELATION TO THE CHURCH COMMUNITY[84]

Worship

In any discussion of the worship of the New Testament church it is as well to keep in mind that 'as for the arrangement and ordering of Christian assemblies, there is not much that can be said for certain.'[85] It is almost impossible to build up a picture of a 'typical' worship service, for there appears to have been room for much variety in patterns of worship and the New Testament gives only, in passing, occasional indications as to how particular practices were carried out within particular communities. We are concerned here, not so much with discovering what actually took place in worship services overall, but only with any differences that can be found in the worship of men and women and with the reasons that are given for supporting such differences. We shall therefore examine in detail the three passages where Paul discusses the question of women in worship.

1 Corinthians 11:2–16

In 1961 C. F. D. Moule wrote of this passage, 'St Paul's strictures...still await a really convincing explanation.'[86] In 1972 G. B. Caird wrote 'It can hardly be said that the passage has yet surrendered its secret.'[87] There are many divergent interpretations of almost every verse, and it is clear that any attempt to investigate the meaning of what Paul[88] says here can be made only with extreme caution.

Two particular problems arise; firstly the fact that some of the words used in this passage are found only very infrequently in Greek generally, so that although their general sense is clear, it is not easy to ascertain their meaning with precision. Secondly there is the fact that in spite of much speculation it is impossible to know with any certainty just what were the customs of the time regarding hair and headgear.

It should be kept in mind as we look at the passage that Paul is writing here to the whole church, to both men and women and that he is writing of something that concerns both equally. Also we must be careful not to isolate this passage from its context. It is normally seen as a completely separate unit, and in so far as it deals with a particular issue it is certainly self-contained; but perhaps the division between this section and the surrounding verses is not quite as definite as it at first appears. Kähler's suggestion that 'do all to the glory of God' (10:31) is the theme throughout, and that 'give no offence to Jews or to Greeks or to the church of God' (10:32) is the 'heading' for the passage right through to 11:16, ought at least to be given consideration.[89]

Interpretations of individual verses within this passage will clearly be influenced by one's understanding of the situation at the church in Corinth to which Paul wrote. Although there are many minor disagreements and variations as to what were the exact viewpoints of the factions involved, there appear to be two main possibilities regarding the background situation in the church which led to this passage being written. We cannot come to a proper conclusion as to which of these possibilities is more likely until we have examined the passage, but as we are again faced with the chicken and egg problem of how far the way we see the whole influences the way we see the parts and vice-versa, it will be helpful at this stage to give an outline of the possible backgrounds to Paul's words.

(1)   A group of women within the church were refusing to 'cover' themselves in worship services. This was seen by some as a deliberate act of rebellion, either against a specific instruction of Paul's teaching on liberty and equality 'in Christ', was concerned against propriety. Others, probably including the women involved, saw it as an expression of their Christian liberty. Paul then writes, trying to reconcile the various factions. He praises them for their keeping of his instructions generally, but says that the rebellious women have strayed on this point. He repeats his insistence that for various theological, moral and cultural reasons, it was necessary for the women to be covered.

(2)   The situation was not one of rebellion, but of a genuine desire to follow Paul's instructions. The church, having accepted Paul's teaching on liberty and equality 'in Christ', was concerned that the 'covering' of women may be seen as a denial of this equality. Some felt that the custom should be abandoned whereas others were concerned that lack of 'covering' was culturally unacceptable. Paul's reply then praises them for holding to his teaching, but points out that the 'covering' can in fact be seen as a reflection of that difference between the sexes that comes from the creation structure and which must be clearly upheld within the church, rather than reflection of any difference or inequality in status, or even as an infringement of liberty. For a woman deliberately to follow a custom appropriate to men was in no way an expression of her liberty. Rather Paul shows that the 'covering' itself can in fact be seen more as a sign of the woman's authority than of subordination, and he restresses the interdependence of the sexes. In their society it was shameful for a woman to be 'uncovered' and therefore Paul gives them permission and even positive encouragement to be covered even when praying and prophesying. He concludes by pointing out that no other church has felt it necessary to abandon the covering custom.

There are those who presuppose the church situations as in (1), yet disagree as to the nature of Paul's reply, but in general these are the two main lines of approach. The vast majority of scholars have accepted without question the approach as outlined in (1).[90] In looking at the passage in detail, we will seek to discover which of these approaches leads to a clearer understanding of the passage as a whole.

1 Cor.11:2 'I commend you because you remember me in everything and maintain the traditions even as I have delivered them to you.' The section thus begins with a note of praise. Paul commends the church for 'maintaining the traditions'. The word used here for tradition, *paradosis*, can refer to traditions in the sense of customs, that is to ways of ordering the Christian life, or it can refer to the principles of the faith, that is to the handed-down doctrines, as it does in 2 Thessalonians 2:15 and 3:6. In this context, both interpretations are possible. It could refer to customs, such as those relating to hairstyles or headgear, or to theological principles such as liberty.

The 'I do not commend you' of verse 17 is clearly intended as a contrast to verse 2, and therefore it would not be right to take verse 2 as sarcastic,[9] as this would make the contrast meaningless. It is usual to interpret verse 2 as Paul praising them generally but pointing out that they have strayed on one point; that is, in spite of their general adherence to his instructions there is one tradition that they have not kept.[92] However, this too gives less point to the contrasting condemnation of verse 17 and also makes it difficult to see what Paul is in fact commending, as the sections immediately before and after this passage are generally critical. There is no indication that verse 2 is anything but sincere, although to take it as such does involve seeing the whole passage as generally approving of their conduct rather than as rebuking.

1 Cor.11:3 'I want you to understand that the head of every man is Christ, the head of a woman is her husband and the head of Christ is God.' This verse has often been taken as the key to an understanding of Paul's thought regarding women. This may be so, but there are certain problems to be resolved before we can decide which lock the key fits! Firstly, the question of what exactly is meant by headship in this context. Secondly, are the three headship pairs, Christ-every man, man-woman, God-Christ to be seen in series or in parallel? That is, do we have here a four-fold hierarchy or is it simply a set of three analogous relationships? Thirdly, who is being referred to here? Does the man-woman pairing relate to men and women generally or to husband and wife, and does 'every man' refer only to Christian men or is it of universal application? And fourthly, is this headship relation of man to woman to be taken as an illustration stating the situation as it exists, or is it a definite statement of theological principle?

All these questions are linked and cannot be dealt with fully in isolation from each other or from the passage as a whole. However, to take the last point first, whether man being the head of woman is an illustration of the Christological statement or a principle in itself seems to depend on whether the passage is seen as having the headship of Christ or the relation of male and female as its major theme. If we take the headship of Christ as the primary theme[93] then the male-female relation can be seen as an illustration of this. However, there is nothing else in the passage referring directly to the headship of Christ, therefore, it does seem better to see the headship relation between men and women as the primary theme. The anthropological statement is firmly placed between the Christological brackets, and these must govern our understanding of its meaning; but this statement is to be seen not as a temporal illustration but as a clear and definite theological principle.

It is normally taken for granted that what headship means, that is, what this theological principle is or implies, is that the man has authority over the woman, but as we have shown on pages 65 to 69, this is an unnecessary and possibly an unwarranted conclusion. It seems preferable here to see Paul's emphasis as being rather on distinction within unity. Support for this is found later in the passage where Paul brings out both the clear distinction between the sexes and also their unity.

The context of the whole passage makes it likely that 'every man' here should be taken as referring to every Christian man and not to man in general,[94] though it is impossible to tell from the verse whether Paul is referring to man-woman generally or to husband-wife.[95] If 'head' is taken as meaning an authoritative leader or ruler, it is easier to see the reference as being to husband-wife, as even in Paul's day there was no question of every woman being under the authority of every man. If head is taken as origin or source, then the reference is more likely to be to man-woman. If headship stresses the unity of the two then both interpretations are possible as both, though in different senses, would be true. (This is an important question as far as the general relationships between men and women are concerned, but it does not actually make much difference to the force of Paul's arguments within this chapter.)

It is clear that Paul is introducing his comments concerning the headgear of the Corinthians by talking about relationships and by stating that there is something distinctive about the relationship between men and women which ought to affect their behaviour. It is something which compares with the distinction in the relationship between Christ and every man and between God and Christ, that is, something absolutely fundamental which they should have kept in mind alongside their desire to 'maintain the traditions' as delivered to them by Paul. However, there is nothing at all to indicate that Paul meant the three pairs to be linked together in terms of a descending ladder.

We have shown that the use of 'head' does not automatically

imply any idea of subordination, and thus the verse cannot be self-evidently held to support a four-fold hierarchy of God-Christ-man-woman. Hurley[96] begins his exegesis of this passage with an assumption of this hierarchy, and often the starting point is to see 'a chain of subordination',[97] a 'ladder of subordination',[98] or a 'descending order of subordination'.[99] Bruce concludes that the essence of headship is origin rather than lordship but still says, 'As to the order of creation, there is a hierarchy of the order; God-Christ-man-woman.'[100]

However, Chrysostom's argument that we cannot see a hierarchy here remains persuasive. He says that if we do 'the Son will be as far removed from the Father as we are from Him. Nay and the woman will be as far removed from us as we are from the Word of God. And what the Son is to the Father, this both we are to the Son and the woman again to the man. And who will endure this?'[101] It is also true that if Paul meant to describe a hierarchy, it is difficult to see any reason why he should choose deliberately to obscure this by beginning in the middle rather than at either end and following the order through. There is therefore no intrinsic reason why the three pairs should not simply be seen as analogous parallels with no idea of a descending hierarchy at all and there is good reason why they should be so seen.

Thus one can identify two major lines of approach to this verse which broadly follow the two approaches outlined on page 83. Either Paul is stressing the distinction between woman and man in order to show that this distinction means that the claim by the Corinthian women to equal rights in worship must be rejected, or he is accepting their claim to equality and emphasising the distinction between the sexes in such a way as to show that though the distinction must be maintained, it does not affect their equality in worship.

1 Cor. 11:4–6 'Any man who prays or prophesies with his head covered dishonours his head, but any woman who prays or prophesies with her head unveiled dishonours her head – it is the same as if her head were shaven. For if a woman will not veil herself, then she should cut off her hair; but if it is disgraceful for a woman to be shorn or shaven, let her wear a veil.'

These verses make it clear that while Paul is arguing in favour of differing customs for men and women regarding headgear, he takes it for granted that their behaviour in relation to prayer and prophecy will be parallel. 'That there was liberty in the church for women to pray is necessarily implied by Paul's argument.'[102] The section loses its point completely if Paul is regulating for something which either did not or should not take place; and there is no hint that Paul thought of the practice as undesirable. Weeks[103] argues that verse 5 should be translated as 'every woman praying and prophesying by means of the unveiling of the head' with the word for uncovering taken as an instrumental dative. That is, he sees prayer and prophecy as only possible when the head is unveiled; it is shameful for a woman to be unveiled, therefore she ought not to pray or prophesy. However, this seems to make nonsense of the parallel in verse 4 which would have to read 'every man praying ... by means of the covering of his head'.

It is impossible for us to state exactly what particular custom is being referred to here. We do not have any conclusive evidence as to the precise nature of the common practice regarding headgear for men and women nor as to what symbolic significance, if any, was accorded to the different customs. The evidence we do have seems to indicate that there was a great deal of variation in different regions and between town and country. The passage itself does not greatly help to clarify what custom Paul has in mind. The only time he in fact uses a specific word which could be translated as 'veil' or 'headcovering' is in verse 15 where we have 'her hair is given to her *instead of* a covering'.[104] The terms used elsewhere in the chapter are all various forms of the same rather obscure word (*akataluptos*) which clearly has some relation to the head and includes the sense of hanging down, but does not necessarily relate to a headcover at all. In fact Hurley argues very convincingly[105] that it cannot be the wearing of a shawl or veil on the head that is the practice being considered here. This would mean that Paul was rejecting Old Testament[106] and Jewish worship customs for men, and surely such a distinct change would have been at least mentioned elsewhere. Paul himself, and indeed Jesus also, often took part in synagogue worship – presumably with covered head. Was this shameful? If the custom referred to is the wearing of a head cover for women but not men we are forced to conclude either that the Old Testament was prescribing a custom which was dishonouring, surely unthinkable; or that the coming of Christ introduced a new distinction between men and women based on a differing relation to God which made the new customs appropriate – surely equally unthinkable when we remember that in Christ 'there is neither male nor female' (Gal. 3:28).

Another relevant point here is that 1 Corinthians 11 is not the only place in the New Testament where instructions are given concerning a woman's hairstyle. 1 Timothy 2:9 and 1 Peter 3:3 both reject the custom of braiding the hair. Remembering that 1 Timothy 2:9 comes in the context of worship, it would appear that instructions relating to hairstyle would be made redundant if it were being taken for granted that all the women would have their heads covered anyway.

If the custom in mind is not then the wearing of a veil, what is it? Hurley translates *akataluptos* as 'unloosed' and puts forward the view that the custom in view for women is the wearing of the hair up in a sort of bun. However, others[107] argue that what is in view is merely the length of hair, with *akataluptos* meaning 'uncovered' – i.e. by long hair. W. J. Martin thinks that it is long hair that Paul is talking about, but he finds it inconceivable that Paul, particularly in the light of chapter 10, could in these verses be forbidding any Christian women, who had, perhaps in her heathen days, been shorn, from participating in worship. Martin therefore sees Paul's use of different tenses in verse 6 as deliberate, so we have 'if a woman is not covered (has not long hair) then let her remain cropped (*keirasthō* – aorist imperative with cessative force referring to a particular situation)... but since it is a shame for a woman to be cropped or shorn let her become covered (i.e. let her hair grow again; *katakaluptesthai* present imperative for a non-terminative inchoative action...).'[108] It may be that the shame of being shorn refers to the public shaving of prostitutes, but although this is a possibility, in this regard also we cannot be completely sure of what the customs were. Perhaps Paul's reference to being shorn is simply that he is telling the women that if they want to be like the men, they might as well go the whole way and make themselves bald. If they do not find this acceptable then let them be covered as the women normally were.

The difficulty in coming to a definite conclusion about the exact nature of the custom described here is perhaps an indication that we should be very wary about claiming biblical support for any insistence on a particular form of headgear in the church today. What is clear in these verses is that Paul is giving strong support to the difference in custom between men and women.

Whatever the custom is, the significance of these verses depends to some extent on whether Paul is using 'head' in its literal sense throughout the verses or whether when he talks of dishonouring the head he is then using it in a metaphorical sense. On the first occasions in verse 4 and verse 5 and on the third occasion in verse 5 it is clearly literal. The second occasion in each verse is normally taken as metaphorical, but this is not self-evidently correct.[109] If it is metaphorical in these instances then the dishonour in question is seen as either (i) a denial of status in the creation order,[110] in which case, while it is fairly easy to see how a man or a woman's denial of the creation as it is would be dishonouring to Christ, it is difficult to see why a denial of this kind by the woman would dishonour the man; or (ii) as by those who see the particular headgear or hairstyle in view as a symbol of authority or submission – a point which is very difficult to substantiate from contemporary literature[111], but is nevertheless possible – the dishonour of the man comes from the woman's denial of his authority over her and the dishonour of Christ from the man's denial of his own authority.[112] It is not easy to see why Christ should be dishonoured by this, unless Hurley's view that Christ is dishonoured by the man's announcing – by covering his head – that he is under the authority of one other than Christ is correct. However, we are still left with the problem of why, if the covering is the symbol of a woman's submission to man, it should not also be seen as the symbol of man's submission to Christ.

Perhaps then it is better to take the head as literal throughout these verses, an approach supported by the subsequent reference to shaving in verse 5.[113] If this is correct, then Paul is saying that to follow a custom which in that society was seen as disgraceful, was dishonouring to a person. It is possible that he is also emphasising the difference between the sexes and the validity of each sex in its own right. For either men or women to follow a custom appropriate to the other sex, means that they are in one sense denying their own sex and thus dishonouring themselves. For a woman to dress her hair as a man would is by no means an expression of liberty. A woman should exercise her freedom to pray and prophesy as a woman, and a man should do so as a man.

1 Cor. 11:7–9 'For a man ought not to cover his head since he is the image and glory of God; but woman is the glory of man. For man was not made from woman but woman from man. Neither was man created for woman but woman for man.'

Because they speak of the creation of woman from and for man, these verses are often taken as evidence that it is the question of the authority of men over women that Paul is stressing here and it is assumed that they therefore provide warrant for seeing an authority structure in verse 3. G. W. Knight states that, 'Paul is saying in effect that it is simply the proper application of concepts and realities to affirm that if one human being is created to be the helper for another human being then the one who receives such help has a certain authority over the one who is his helper.'[114] Similarly, Fisher concludes that these verses are 'Paul's interpretation of the fact that woman's creation was secondary...her function in life was to show the authority and supremacy of men.'[115] However, there is no indication in the verses that this is what Paul is saying, and it is certainly not supported by Genesis.[116]

G. B. Caird, because he believes that these verses do reflect

Paul's sincere belief that the subjection of women was based on the creation order, accuses him of faulty logic and faulty exegesis of Genesis.[117] However, this presupposes that Paul sees the veil as a symbol of authority and that he is using the 'creation order' in order to provide a theological argument that woman is under the authority of the man and therefore ought to wear the symbol of this authority. If on the other hand Paul is quoting from Genesis and stressing the creation differences simply in order to emphasize that woman was created different from man, and that she can therefore worship as a woman, without any need to imitate man, then most of the difficulties over Paul's exegesis of Genesis are removed.

There are those who see in verse 7 a statement of Paul's opinion that woman is the image of God only in a secondary sense.[118] However, this would not only clearly contradict the teaching of Genesis but would also create very real difficulties regarding teaching elsewhere in the New Testament on the unity of mankind 'in Adam' and of the church 'in Christ'. In any case, Paul does not directly say this, and it seems likely that there is a deliberate choice of words, 'image and glory' (verse 7) rather than 'image and likeness' (Genesis 1:26) and a lack of repetition of the word 'image' to avoid this implication. Feuillet interprets the verse as in fact ennobling women, for she is not only, like the man, the image of God, but she is also the glory of man;[119] though this does seem to be reading as much into the verses as does the interpretation of those who take it for granted that Paul is stressing the subservience of women.

Thus though it is possible that Paul included these verses in order to remind the women of their subordinate place and this possibility remains even if the implication of women not being the image of God is rejected; it is equally possible that in verses 4–9 Paul is supporting the covering of women and stressing the differences in the creation of men and women in order to emphasize that the equality of women with men before God does not mean identity, but that women are free to worship as women. If this latter interpretation is correct, then verse 10 follows on naturally from these verses.

1 Cor. 11:10 'That is why a woman ought to have authority on her head, because of the angels.' The woman should for these reasons accept the covering custom as an indication of her new found authority as a woman. Some have taken the 'authority' (*exousia*) as the authority of the husband over the wife,[120] but this is extremely unlikely as there is no parallel for *exousia* being used in the passive sense that would be necessary if this interpretation were correct, and there is nothing in the context to indicate that the word was being used in anything other than the normal way.[121] There is certainly no warrant at all for the replacement, as in the RSV, of *exousia* by the word *'veil'*. Paul's Greek readers would never have understood it in this way in spite of the possible, if rather obscure, word-play which could link the word for veil and the word for authority to the same Aramaic root.[122]

Hurley thinks that so far Paul has stressed subordination but he recognizes that here at least the emphasis is on the authority of the woman herself. As Banks points out, 'Once again, as in 1 Corinthians 7:1–4, the wife is recognized as possessing a legitimate sphere of authority alongside her husband.'[123]

The interpretation of the second half of verse 10 is notoriously difficult, partly because the evidence that is available concerning the early Jewish attitude to angels is somewhat mixed. In general there are four possibilities as to what is meant by 'because of the angels'.[124]

i) They are fallen angels, parallel to those in Genesis 6:2. Women must then be covered in order to protect them from the advances of such angels. This view, although held by Tertullian, is now largely discounted.

ii) They are 'representatives and guardians of the old pagan world order'.[125] Women therefore should wear a sign of their authority 'out of deference to the accepted conventions of the society in which she lives.' That is, as long as the old order remains, under the guardianship of angels, its customs must be followed.[126]

iii) They are good angels who are present during worship. Fitzmeyer uses evidence from the Qumran literature to support the idea of angels as present during sacred gatherings. 'Because of the angels' then means 'out of reverence for the angels' who are present and who should not look on the uncovered women, either because to be uncovered was shameful, or because man's glory should be hidden in the presence of God and his angels.[127] Linked with this is the view that sees the angels as guardians of the 'creation order'. Men and women were created differently, and the angels are concerned to see that that difference is not negated even in the new age.

iv) A fourth possibility is that there may be some link between the authority of the women, mentioned here, and the judging of angels as in 1 Corinthians 6:3. However, as Héring reminds us, we know so little about the ideas of the time concerning angels that it is almost impossible to come to a definite conclusion as to the meaning here.[128]

If verses 3–9 are seen as emphasising that a woman as woman is free to worship, and that to follow the customs of that society which were appropriate to the men is quite the reverse of an expression of Christian liberty, then verse 10, emphasising her authority, provides a natural link with verses 11–12. If, on the other hand, verses 3–9 are seen as stressing the need for women to maintain a subordinate role, then verse 10, showing that this subordination does not in any way remove the authority of the woman in worship,[129] becomes the necessary transition between these verses and verses 11–12.

1 Cor. 11:11   'Nevertheless in the Lord woman is not independent of man nor man of woman.' Paul here states that, in spite of the differences between men and women, which because they are part of the creation structure must not and in fact cannot be negated, nevertheless the two sexes are interdependent and their independent authority cannot alter that. Men and women, not only in the family, but also in the church, need one another. Bailey notes the implication of this verse that even those who follow Paul's advice in chapter 7 and remain celibate must not ignore or set aside this relation of interdependence between the sexes.[130] It does not seem as if Paul would have been very much in favour of single sex communities.

1 Cor. 11:12   'For as woman was made from man, so man is now born of woman and all things are of God.'

This verse is often taken as a corrective parallel to verses 8–9, so that Paul, having in the earlier verses stressed the man's superiority, is now showing that they must be careful not to take this too far. However, it seems more logical to see verse 12 as pointing to the fact that Paul had no intention of the earlier verses implying the subordination or the inferiority of woman. Rather, 'all things are of God'. Both men and women, remembering their dependence on each other, and their reversal of roles in creation and procreation, should nevertheless in all things look first to God, who created both and who now redeems both.

Kähler suggests that these two verses rather than verse 3 should be seen as the keystone of the whole passage, with verse 3 'rightly understood' being already an indication to verses 11–12. It is probably better to view these verses in their place as part of a logically developed argument, for they clearly are part of that argument and not merely a parenthesis, as the brackets found in some versions makes them appear.

1 Cor. 11:13   'Judge for yourselves, is it proper for a woman to pray to God with her head uncovered?'

Paul returns now to the Corinthians' question. He has presented his arguments and his 'judge for yourselves' does not mean that this is an open question on which the Corinthians were entitled to make up their own minds; rather he is suggesting that in the light of what he has said so far the answer is clear.

1 Cor. 11:14–15 'Does not nature itself teach you that for a man to wear long hair is degrading to him, but if a woman has long hair it is her pride? For her hair is given to her instead of a covering.'

These verses confirm the fact that whatever the custom concerned is, it is not the wearing of a veil, for verse 15 clearly states that the woman's hair is given instead of a veil.[131] It is not obvious what Paul means by 'nature' in verse 14. The examples of Samson, Absalom, or even the Stoics, of which Paul must have been aware, show that there is no biological difference in hair length between male and female. Barrett's suggestion that underlying Paul's thoughts here is a horror of homosexuality[132] has much to commend it.

Maybe Paul is saying in verses 14 and 15, 'I have explained why following this custom is acceptable and desirable, but in any case don't you feel in your bones that not to follow it is degrading?' Woman's hair is her glory, making her like a man does not add any honour to her at all. However, perhaps Caird is right when he says that 'whatever lesson Paul expected his readers to derive from Mother Nature it is one which eludes the modern reader.'[133]

1 Cor. 11:16 'If any one is disposed to be contentious, we recognize no other practice, nor do the churches of God.'

It is possible that the 'other practice' here refers to the 'being contentious' of the first half of the verse,[134] so Paul is saying that neither himself nor the churches will tolerate contention on a point of this kind. A similar view is that of J. C. Greig who translates this verse as, 'we have more to do than argue, rather than provoke contentiousness we have no custom the one way or the other, either personally or as churches.'[135] It does seem more likely, though, that the practice in question relates to the custom that has been referred to throughout the section. If so, then it is usually assumed that Paul is appealing to the general practice of the church as a final argument against those who will not accept the previous discussion, or as an extra argument[136], because he himself is not really convinced by what he has said so far. Kähler takes this latter view,[137] seeing Paul finding himself on uncertain ground, as falling back on dictatorial assertion.

However, if the Corinthians' original question was in the form, 'Does this covering custom negate women's equality with men before God and should we therefore not allow them to be covered?', then Paul here brings his argument to a close by saying that neither he nor any of the other churches have found it necessary to flout convention in this way, and there is no reason why the Corinthians should do so.

So then let us return to the question of what the particular problem of the church in Corinth was. Our understanding of the passage depends to some extent on whether we see the background situation in the church as being:

i) That certain women were flouting convention and possibly Paul's direct instructions in order to claim an equality of status that was not rightly theirs, or

ii) That they were worried that by following convention women were denying the equality of status with men that was now theirs in Christ.

If we accept the former approach, then it appears that Paul is agreeing that the women must signify their subordination by being covered in worship, though he does stress that this does not alter their authority to worship or to take part in prayer and prophecy. If the latter approach is correct, then Paul is agreeing that women are free and equal but stating that this freedom and equality is not in fact denied by covering so that they are quite free to follow the custom, as indeed all the other churches do.

I would suggest that this latter approach is in fact more likely for the following reasons.

i) It makes more sense of Paul's praise in verse 2 and also makes it easier to interpret the word 'tradition' in the way it is used elsewhere in the New Testament.

ii) The word 'subordination' and like forms do not occur in the passage. The only place where the concept could possibly be identified is in verse 3 and we have shown that even here it is by no means necessarily implied.

iii) It removes the problem of Paul's use of theological principles to support the maintenance of one particular, cultural convention.

iv) It invalidates the accusation that Paul is using faulty logic and faulty exegesis of Genesis.

v) It fits in better with Paul's views expressed elsewhere on liberty 'in Christ'. If subordination of women to men is to be emphasized even in worship, it is difficult to see how 'neither male nor female' can be given any real meaning at all.

vi) It sees a development through the whole passage and makes it sound less like the discussion of a philosophical school.[138]

vii) It follows more easily from the context of chapter 10.

Thus Paul in this chapter is supporting the equality of women in worship and their full participation in prayer and prophecy. He points out that this equality does not imply a necessity for a false identity between the sexes, and that there is no reason therefore to overthrow any conventions of dress that emphasize their distinction. It must be noted that basically Paul is supporting the status quo in terms of conventions. There is possibly a built-in principle of liberation within this chapter but Paul does not argue here for a quick removal of the subordination or the inferiority of women in society.

1 Corinthians 14:34–36[139]

'The women should keep silence in the churches. For they are not permitted to speak but should be subordinate, as even the law says. If there is anything they desire to know, let them ask their husbands at home. For it is shameful for a woman to speak in church. What! Did the word of God originate with you, or are you the only ones it has reached?'

There are certain initial questions that arise from this passage and which must be taken into account in any interpretations. (i) To take these verses as an absolute prohibition of a woman ever taking any vocal part in public worship brings an immediate conflict with chapter 11:5. (ii) It is very difficult to find any Old Testament passages bearing a direct relation to the instructions given here, and in any case the appeal to the law sounds strangely unlike Paul. (iii) How can verse 35 be related to unmarried women, widows, and those with non-Christian husbands? (iv) The rebuke in verse 36 is very strong and we need to make sense of the severity of that rebuke. Keeping these problems in mind, let us look at the four main lines of approach to the interpretation of this passage.

(a) These verses are sometimes seen as a non-Pauline interpolation, probably written by the author of 1 Timothy 2 which is then also seen as non-Pauline. This is the view taken by Conzelmann[140] who thinks that this section 'upsets the context, because it interrupts the theme of prophecy and spoils the flow of thought'. He notes the contradiction with chapter 11 and comes to the conclusion that 'in this regulation we have a reflection of the bourgeois consolidation of the Church, roughly on the level of the Pastoral epistles.' However, while a small group of manuscripts[141] do transfer verses 34 and 35 to a position after verse 40, most of the evidence is against this transferral and there is no evidence at all to indicate that these verses were ever absent altogether. If these verses were a later interpolation it is strange that no evidence of this remains. As far as their possible placing after verse 40 is concerned, while it is understandable that the verses should be removed from here to follow verse 40, there seems to be no reason at all why, if their correct place is after verse 40, they should have been replaced between verse 33 and verse 36.

To treat these verses as non-Pauline would certainly remove the problems of interpretation, but we have to agree with Barrett that 'the textual evidence is not quite strong enough to make it compelling.'[142] Thus it seems that these verses are an integral part of the passage in which they stand and must be interpreted within that context.

(b) Some assume that Paul is commanding total silence for all women in all church services, so that we have 'an absolute prohibition against women's speaking'.[143] This view led Grosheide to conclude that chapter 11 cannot refer to public services. However, we have shown that this conclusion is unlikely (cf p.86 above) even if it were possible to show that the New Testament does maintain a clear distinction between public and private worship, something which is at the very least, debatable. Jewett recognizes that chapter 11 refers to public worship, yet agrees that what is being required here is total silence. He therefore understands chapter 11 and chapter 14 as being in unresolved conflict. The former is seen as reflecting the impetus of the new covenant, and the latter as a hang-over reflecting Paul's Jewish scruples. He sees all of the interpretations described in section (c) below as introducing a false harmonization.[144] However, it is very difficult to accept that a man of Paul's calibre would not have recognized such a contradiction in his writing and made at least some attempt to show the Corinthians how two contradictory views could be held together.

The conflict with 11:5 is not the only problem with this approach. If verse 34 is an absolute prohibition then this has far-reaching implications for the interpretation of the rest of the chapter. It means that verse 26, 'when you come together, each one has a hymn, a lesson, a revelation, a tongue or an interpretation ', must be seen as applying only to the men of the church and not to the women. There is no indication apart from verses 34–35 that this should be so, and in fact it can be taken this way only if the whole of chapters 12–14 are seen as excluding women, which is at the least unlikely. This in turn would create serious difficulties of interpretation for the whole of the New Testament; decisions would have to be made as to when women are to be excluded from instructions and exhortations given to Christians generally and a real division between the sexes would be created regarding their relationship to God, a division which makes a nonsense of the concept of unity in Christ.

Robertson and Plummer[145] recognize that if absolute silence is required then the rest of chapter 14 cannot apply to women and suggest that women 'would join in the "Amen" (verse 16) but otherwise not be heard'. However, it is completely arbitrary to decide that verse 16 applies to women but not verse 26. L. Birney[146] makes a telling point here when, acknowledging that the Old Testament nowhere forbids women to speak in the assembly, he questions whether we can use a passage based on the law to forbid something which is never forbidden by the law. In fact even the Rabbinic law, though having a distinct preference for the non-participation of women, never completely forbids them from taking any part at all. Thus the problems involved in this approach to the passage means that it is not really tenable as an interpretation.

(c) The majority of modern scholars take the view that what Paul requires is not total silence, but the limitation of some particular form of participation. There is a great variety of opinions as to what form that limitation should take. We will consider here four of the most widely held possibilities.

1. Directly inspired speech, such as prayer, prophecy and presumably tongue speaking, is permitted, but all other speech, for example, prepared teaching or asking questions is not.[147] This does avoid conflict with chapter 11 but the other problems remain. In any case the whole context of the passage is dealing with instructions regarding the regulation of inspired speech and it seems very likely that these verses too should be seen in that context.

2. The parallel with verse 28, where in regard to tongue speaking without an interpreter present we have 'let each of them keep silent', and the use of the verb *lalein* 'to speak', often used in the context of tongue speaking, are sometimes seen as indications that what Paul is forbidding here is tongue-speaking by women.[148] Verse 36 then condemns them for claiming superior private revelation. However, unless one presupposes an emotional instability in women, it is difficult to understand why this should apply to women but not to men. Similarly, where does the law come in, why should speaking in tongues be seen as shameful, and what is meant by the reference to questioning their husbands at home? Again the problems raised by this interpretation seem greater than the problems it solves.

3. Another popular interpretation is that which sees verse 35 as providing the key to an understanding of the passage. 'The problem is clearly one of interruption of the meetings by questions from the wives.'[149] It is true that if it were something more than this it is

hard to see why Paul should single out this one aspect. Stendahl[150] thinks that verse 35 'makes it clear that the silence stands in contrast to 'asking questions' not to preaching, teaching or prophesying'. These questions may have been in the form of noisy chatter between themselves, of cross-talk, perhaps across the room, with their husbands, or as part of the section of worship when the prophecies were debated (verse 29). In each of these cases, it is difficult to see how such statements as 'they are not permitted to speak' and 'it is shameful' could be understood as meaning no more than this.[151] It is also difficult to see why the rebuke in verse 36 should be so strong. However verse 35 indicates that the prohibition does refer in some way to the questioning of husbands by their wives.

4.   Others see the key phrase as 'but they should be subordinate', though they come to different conclusions as to how it should be applied.

(i) L. Birney[152] states that 'teaching is by nature an exercise of authority and would violate the principle of submission of women to men, and therefore Paul must be referring to teaching here. By 'the law' Paul is assumed to be referring to either Genesis 3:16, or else Genesis 1–2 or 1–3 in general. Difficulties remain in that the question of teaching never arises in Genesis 1–3, that subordination is by no means self-evident in these chapters and that Genesis 3:16 is not a command but a prediction.[153] Also, there is nothing in the context here to show that Paul is referring specifically to teaching and again verse 35 would be difficult to fit into this interpretation.

(ii) J. Hurley[154] takes a similar line but he sees these verses as a commentary on verse 29, 'Let two or three prophets speak and let the others weigh what is said.' Women were taking part in judgment of the prophets and thus were 'assuming the anomalous role of judging man.' Paul commands them not to do this. The shame then refers to women taking part in public debate. Certain problems relating to the position of unmarried women and the meaning of verse 36 remain, but this explanation does take note of the context and has some plausibility, particularly if verse 36 is seen as beginning a new paragraph, as Hurley suggests.

(iii) E. Kähler[155] sees the subordination referred to here as not to men, but rather to the order of worship. This would then fit in with the whole emphasis on order that prevails throughout the chapter. The woman must avoid whatever unseemly behaviour had been disturbing the order of worship in Corinth. It is quite possible that subordination here does refer to the church and its order rather than to men, but again it is difficult to see why this should apply to women only.

All these explanations leave us with the problem of the un-married women, widows and those whose husbands are not Christian. Fisher notes this problem and says, 'Paul dealt only in general principles.' However, this is not true elsewhere, as for example in 1 Corinthians 7 where Paul specifically takes note of differing minority groups. Barrett[156] sees Paul as assuming 'a fortiori, un-married women and wives of unbelievers will not speak,' and that they must ask their friends to ask their husbands. However, this seems to conflict with Paul's attitude to unmarried women in 1 Corinthians 7. Another major problem in this area is that the forbidding of women to ask questions in public conflicts strongly with the line taken by Jesus who found no difficulty in debating with women in the presence of his male followers.[157] However, both these problems can be solved if we take Hurley's interpreta-tion ((c) 4.iii) a little further and assume that what is being prohibited is not the questioning of any man by any woman, but a wife taking part in the judging of her own husband.

(d) A rather different way of dealing with the problems raised by these verses is to assume that verses 34 and 35 are not in fact expressing Paul's own opinion but are quoting, perhaps directly from a letter, the views of one group within the church.[158] Verse 36 is then Paul's strong repudiation of these views. In this instance 'the law' is seen as the Jewish oral law. It is certainly easier to relate this passage to such statements from the Jewish law as 'a woman may speak to no man other than her husband' (M. Ket 7:6) or that a woman should not read from the Torah 'out of respect for the congregation' (Meg. 23a) than it is to find any equivalent statement in the Law of Moses or indeed in the Old Testament at all. S. Aalen[159] shows that the phrase 'for they are not permitted' is part of the technical vocabulary of Judaism. We know that Paul on other occasions does use this pattern of quoting from their letter and then refuting what they have said (as for example in 1 Corinthians 6:12ff), although one should note that there is no other instance of a quotation quite as long as this one would be.

If this interpretation is correct then verses 26–40 form a contin-uous section following on from the rest of the chapter. After laying stress on the order which is necessary in worship, Paul has said, 'You can all prophesy one by one, so that all may learn and all be encouraged' (verse 31). He then brings in the opinion of those Judaisers who feel that such participation should be the prerogative of men, and rebukes them indignantly. 'What! Did the word of God originate with you, or are you the only ones it has reached?'

(verse 36). It is not the Jewish oral law but rather what Paul writes that is the command of the Lord (verse 37). Keeping in mind his main theme that 'all things should be done decently and in order' (verse 40), they should all 'earnestly desire to prophesy and not forbid speaking in tongues' (verse 39).

The transposition of verses 34–35 in the Western texts shows that they were linked together and makes feasible the possibility that they are a separate quote. This interpretation removes the problems outlined above and does make sense within the context. However, one problem does remain. If this view is correct, why from early times has there been a consistent misunderstanding of the passage?

It seems to me that if we are to take verses 34–36 seriously within their context we are left with two possible options. Either they should be seen as reflecting not Paul's own opinion, but that of a particular faction within the church at Corinth with whom Paul then disagrees. This view, while not without its own problems does provide a satisfactory explanation of all the factors involved. Or, if these verses are to be seen as expressing Paul's own opinion, then the fewest number of difficulties is involved if they are seen as referring to a prohibition of wives taking part in the public discussion of prophecies made by their own husbands.

In either case, it is difficult to dispute the comment made by Calvin on verse 40, 'This statement shows that he did not wish to bind consciences by the foregoing precepts as if they were in themselves necessary, but only in so far as they were subservient to propriety and peace.'[160]

1 Timothy 2:8–15[161]

While the contention of B. W. Powers that 'we should see the primary reference of this passage as being to a marriage situation, not public worship,'[162] is possible, the continuing theme of prayer and the use of 'in every place', in verse 8, make it likely that the section refers also to behaviour in a wider sphere than the home.[163] Certainly the way in which this passage has been used to regulate the role of women in public worship justifies an examination of its contents at this point.

1 Tim. 2:8–10   'I desire then that in every place the men should pray, lifting holy hands without anger or quarreling; also that women should adorn themselves modestly and sensibly in seemly apparel, not with braided hair or gold or pearls or costly attire but by good deeds as befits women who profess religion.'

There are those who see in verse 8 the implication that men only should pray[164], but verses 8 and 9 are grammatically linked, so that the 'also' – a better translation of *ōsautōs* would be 'likewise' – of verse 9 should be supplemented with 'I wish them to pray.'[165] The word 'apparel' can refer to dress, but it can also refer to attitude or character; thus the emphasis here is on the manner in which prayer should be made, that is with an attitude of respect and without ostentation. To see verse 8 as forbidding women to pray would mean that we are presented with a direct parallel between prayer for men and dress for women; a parallel which is not immediately obvious nor seems to be in line with the thought of Paul elsewhere.

Note again Paul's concern here that in worship everything should be done decently and in order. Perhaps the men at Ephesus had a tendency to use the opportunity given by public prayer to further their own quarrels and the women had a tendency to show off, Paul puts both of them right.

1 Tim. 2:11 'Let a woman learn in silence with all submissiveness.'

We know from 2 Timothy 3:5–7 that there was a particular tendency towards heresy in some of the Ephesian women. This is perhaps not surprising in view of the lack of education of women and their lack of training in discerning truth. Spencer[166] suggests that certain men were implying that all women were like Eve, transgressors by nature and should not even be allowed to learn. This would certainly reflect the Jewish attitude of the time. Paul then here is making a positive statement that the women should be allowed to learn, and he also points out in verse 14 that Eve became a transgressor, rather than being one by nature.

It should be made clear here that the word *hēsuchia* can mean 'silence' as the RSV translates it, but it can also simply mean quietness. It is used this way in 1 Timothy 2:2 and also in 2 Thessalonians 3:12 where in both cases 'silence' would be a completely inappropriate translation. Here too it is probably better to translate it as 'quietness', particularly if the word *manthanetō* 'to learn' has the sense it sometimes has of learning especially by enquiry.[167] 'All submissiveness' in this instance probably primarily reflects the attitude required towards the congregation in general, rather than to 'what the men in the congregation teach'[168], although this would clearly be included. There is certainly no indication here that there is a particular submission required from all women to all men, other than that which is generally required from every Christian to every other. Ward suggests that the phrase implies that 'women may not choose the subjects in which they are willing to be taught'[169] but this appears a little far-fetched. It may be that to learn 'in quietness with all submission' in fact reflects the educational ideas of the time regarding the best way of learning. Certainly the radical nature of Paul's insistence that the women should learn must not be forgotten. He was again refuting contemporary social attitudes by implying that women's 'role as homemakers did not fulfil the ultimate priority for which they were created'.[170] Christian women were required not only to sit back and listen, but also to learn.

1 Tim. 2:12 'I permit no woman to teach or to have authority over men; she is to keep silent.'

Spencer sees the particle *de*, which is omitted by RSV and NEB and is normally, although by no means always adversative (that is, it is more often than not best translated as 'but' although in many cases 'and' is a perfectly acceptable translation), as bringing out a contrast between the learning of verse 11 and the not teaching of verse 12. However, to suggest as she does that Paul used this particle because 'he indubitably knew that the ... two injunctions would eventually be contradictory'[171] cannot be more than a somewhat unlikely conjecture.

There are those who assume that these verses are an absolute prohibition of any woman ever teaching or being in a position of authority over any man, and sometimes even of taking any vocal part in worship, although the probable translation of *hēsuchia* here too as 'quiet' rather than as 'silent' makes this letter far less likely. They then see verses 13 and 14 as basing this prohibition on the structure of creation and thus justifying its absolute nature.[172] However, as we shall see, the particular words used in verse 12 and the explanatory reasons of verses 13 and 14 can just as easily be seen as imposing a limitation on the extent of the prohibition as justifying its absolute nature.

Paul uses the first person singular present indicative active 'I am not permitting' rather than the more formal, 'It is not permitted'. It may be that by doing this Paul is stating that he is using his own personal judgment to say that at the present time he does not give permission for a woman to teach. However, since the verb could be used also to indicate a permanent continuing prohibition, only the context can tell us which is more likely. It may be that local reasons unknown to us, necessitated a specific instruction of this kind; it 'may have been due to the greater facility with which contemporary women were falling under the influence of impostors'.[173] (2 Timothy 3:5–7)

What then is it that Paul is not permitting here? His use of the singular forms of both 'woman' and 'man' (obscured by the RSV's translation 'men') may mean that he is envisaging only the particular situation of a wife teaching her husband[174] and we should translate as, 'I do not permit a wife to teach or have authority over a husband', although the likelihood of this is somewhat lessened by the omission of any possessive pronoun. Whether this is so or not, that the authority mentioned here is directly related to teaching and not to all forms of authority[175] is indicated by the fact that in certain cases wives are specifically described as having authority over their husbands (1 Corinthians 7:4) and that women could hold a position involving some authority within the church (as Phoebe, Romans 16:1, cf p.125–6 below.). In this regard the use of the strong verb *authentein*[176] rather than the more usual *exousiazein* gives clarification to Paul's meaning.

The noun *authentēs* from which this verb comes originally meant suicide, and while this idea dropped out and the sense of master or autocrat became prominent the idea of totally self-directed behaviour remains. Thomas Magister[177] instructs his pupils to use another verb *autodikein* in preference to *authentein*, as this latter was seen as a slang term. *Autodikein* had the meaning of 'to judge by one's own standards' or 'to act on one's own authority' which confirms the element of 'self-willed arbitrary behaviour'[178] or 'self-assured firm conduct'[179] in *authentein*.

Paul is then prohibiting the women (or perhaps the wives) of Ephesus not from holding any form of authority, but from usurping an authority that was not rightly theirs and from domineering over the men by their teaching. Anderson goes as far as to say that 'the manner in which the wife must not instruct her husband is the subject dealt with. It is not the question of instructing or teaching him but the manner of doing it.'[180] 1 Timothy 1:7 tells us that there were those in the church at Ephesus who wanted to be teachers but who did not have the necessary understanding and who went about it in quite the wrong way. It seems likely that some of the women formed part of this group and Paul was insisting that they must gain understanding before they can impart it.

1 Tim. 2:13 'For Adam was formed first, then Eve.' Paul is often seen as introducing two arguments to show why a woman teaching a man is 'contrary to natural order'.[181] Firstly, it is assumed that in stating the chronological priority of Adam's creation Paul is arguing that this 'places him in a position of superiority over women'[182] as 'the one formed first is to have dominion'.[183] However, while it is possible to draw this inference the New Testament never in fact does so, and we have shown[184] that it is not a necessary inference from Genesis. Calvin says of this verse, 'The reason which Paul assigns, that woman was second in the order of creation, appears not to be a very strong argument in favour of her subjection.'[185] In any case, even if in this verse Paul is meaning to emphasize the subjection of women, it is not immediately obvious what relevance this has for the interpretation of verse 12. It is usually taken for granted that teaching, unlike prophecy, is a particularly authoritative function, but this distinction is not very easy to maintain from the New Testament evidence, as it is prophecy that seems to be given the greater status. Perhaps this statement of the priority of Adam's creation is not being used as a separate argument at all but merely as an introduction to the argument about the deception of Eve.

1 Tim. 2:14 '... and Adam was not deceived, but the woman was deceived and became a transgressor.' The meaning of this verse has again often been taken as self-evident. 'The tragedy of the fall establishes the general truth that a woman is more easily deceived than a man.'[186] Therefore Paul is seen as deducing that 'women are by nature so easily deceived that they can never be trusted to teach.'[187] But is this really what Paul is intending to say by his use of this illustration? Or is the interpretation a deduction based more on a particular view of psychology resulting from an Aristotelian world-view,[188] than on what the text actually says here or indeed on what is said elsewhere in Scripture? It is difficult to find any scriptural warrant for Hendriksen's comment on these verses. 'In his sovereign wisdom God made the human pair in such a manner that it is natural for him to lead, for her to follow; for him to be aggressive, for her to be receptive; for him to invent, for her to use the tools which he invents. The tendency to follow was embedded in Eve's very soul as she came forth from the hand of her creator.'[189]

There are two major reasons for questioning the interpretation of Paul's words as a reflection on the nature of woman as such, introduced in order to support an absolute ban on their giving any teaching. Firstly, in 2 Corinthians 11:3 Paul uses the same illustration of the deception of Eve to talk of the possibility of both male and female members of the church being deceived in the way that Eve was.[190] Thus while Paul is clearly drawing some comparison between Eve's having been deceived and the women at Ephesus, it seems unlikely that he thought of such a tendency as being an integral part of the nature of woman as opposed to man.

Secondly, and perhaps more importantly, if the reason why women are not to teach is that they are easily deceived and cannot therefore be trusted, then the fact that they are permitted to teach children and other women (2 Timothy 1:5; 3:14; Titus 2:3–4, etc.) would appear to show a lack of concern that these should 'come to a knowledge of the truth' (1 Timothy 2:4), which seems alien to the whole spirit of the New Testament. Surely, if Paul was using the argument in this way, he would have barred women from teaching at all and not simply from teaching men. If, on the other hand, he wanted merely to stress that there is something in the way in which they were created that makes it improper for a man to be taught by a woman, then why bring in the question of deceit at all? It is perhaps surprising that commentators who think that the verse should be interpreted in this way make no attempt to answer these questions.

N. J. Hommes points out the close connection in Paul's thought between possessing wisdom/knowledge, and exercising the teaching/admonishing function in the church[191], a connection which is clearly illustrated in 1 Timothy 1:3–7. Eve had been deceived and had sought to teach Adam something which she herself did not understand. Paul wanted to prevent a recurrence of this, so while the women were in danger of being deceived, perhaps because of their lack of education and knowledge, he forbade them to teach. In particular he forbade them to influence the men, who, by the nature of their society, would be the natural leaders in the church community. As Spencer puts it, 'In their similarity to Eve, the women at Ephesus should neither teach nor have authority over men but they should learn in submission to the constituted authority...of the church.' Spencer then concludes that 'Paul never meant for women to remain at the beginning stage of growth exemplified by women at Ephesus' for 'when women anywhere... grow beyond a resemblance to Eve in this respect, then the analogy is no longer valid.'[192]

There are two further reasons for thinking it unlikely that these verses were ever intended to be taken as an absolute prohibition. Firstly, Timothy was well aware of the way in which Paul had worked freely with many women, some of whom are described as 'labouring in the gospel' with him.[193] Timothy himself had travelled with Paul when Priscilla, who we know had taken part in teaching a man, was one of the party. It is unlikely therefore that Timothy would assume that Paul meant in verse 12 to convey a permanent and universal prohibition.

Secondly, and again probably more importantly, there are many verses in the epistles where the believers are described as teaching, or exhorted to teach, one another.[194] There is no indication at all in the context of these verses to indicate that they are not meant to apply to all believers, male and female alike. If, because of the interpretation of 1 Timothy 2:12 as an absolute prohibition, these verses must be seen as not relevant to women in spite of there being no indication in the context that this is so, then grave hermeneutical difficulties are raised as to just which of Paul's exhortations, addressed apparently to the church as a whole do not apply to women. This is not simply a verbal quibble. It affects our whole attitude to an understanding of Scripture and its authority and is a very real problem particularly for those women who sincerely want to live by scriptural principles.

One can, of course, assume that the teaching being referred to in 1 Timothy is official teaching taking place in the context of a worship service, or specifically authorised by the church, whereas elsewhere what is meant is the general instruction of one believer by another, so that in fact, no contradiction arises. However, it is not clear how far such a definite distinction between official and unofficial teaching can be substantiated from the New Testament, and in any case to introduce such a distinction in itself imposes an arbitrary limitation on the nature of the prohibition here and creates further difficulties for the application of verses 13 and 14.

Thus, the particular words (the strong verb for a domineering authority, and the use of 'I do not permit' rather than the more general 'it is not permitted') and the arguments Paul uses in this section mean that it is not inherently necessary to see in these verses an absolute prohibition of any woman ever teaching or having any kind of authority over any man, or even, if these verses are meant to be limited to the context of marriage, of any wife ever teaching her husband. The words and practice of Paul elsewhere make it most unlikely that they should be seen in this way.

However, it must be noted that while the prohibition is not absolute, it remains a prohibition. No believer, male or female, has an automatic right to teach. Any, particularly women, who are untaught and easily deceived, must continue to concentrate on learning rather than on usurping an authority which has not been given to them.

1 Tim. 2:15 'Yet woman will be saved through bearing children, if she continues in faith and love and holiness, with modesty.'

There is much ambiguity about this verse and most scholars would agree with Barrett[195] that no definite answer can be given as to its meaning. In fact the verse bears no relation to the activities of women in worship and therefore we will consider it here only briefly. Guthrie[196] lists the four major suggestions that have been made as to how the verse should be understood, but it is generally recognized that all of these present some difficulties.

a) Woman will get safely through childbirth, if she continues to live a holy life. The major problem here is the number of cases where this manifestly did not happen.

b) Women will be saved if their children continue in the faith.[197]

This uses the alternative 'if they continue' (RSV margin). The problem with this interpretation is that it is in conflict with what is taught elsewhere about salvation by faith, as it makes the salvation of the woman dependent in some way on the behaviour of her child.

c) Woman will be saved 'by means of the child-bearing' (RV) or 'by the birth of the child', that is, by the birth of Christ. This is a fairly popular explanation and would remove the problems of other interpretations, but it is unlikely to be correct simply because it is a long way from being the most obvious interpretation of the words used and it is strange that if this is what Paul intended to say, he expressed himself in such an obscure and ambiguous fashion.

d) Women will be saved, even though they must bear children. That is, that the effects of the Fall on the child-bearing of women have no bearing on their salvation. The problem here is that 'even though' is a very unnatural translation of the word *dia* 'through'.

Maybe Hommes is right[198] to link this verse with verses 9–10 and to see Paul's concern as 'to uphold the ideal of the Christian housewife'. Paul is certainly against any lessening of the dignity or value of marriage or child-bearing. Whatever a woman's role is elsewhere, her role as a wife and mother is not to be despised. Ward's suggestion[199] that, after the mention of Eve's deception, verse 15 is added so as to avoid any possibility of the thought being left in the air that child-bearing is merely a punishment, also deserves consideration.

Woman in Worship: Conclusion

Thus, Paul, in the passages where the position of woman in worship is considered, shows clearly that sexual differentiation is part of God's creation, and rejects any false identification of the sexes. A woman will worship as a woman, and a man will worship as a man. Nevertheless, there is very little to suggest that Paul advocated specific differences in the activities of men and women as such when the church met together for worship. Both could take part in prayer, in prophecy and in singing (1 Corinthians 11:4–5; 1 Timothy 2:8–9; Ephesians 5:19; Colossians 3:16), both could bring 'a hymn, a lesson, a revelation, a tongue or an interpretation' (1 Corinthians 14:26).

If Paul is giving his own views in 1 Corinthians 14:34–35, then we have a prohibition of wives taking part in the discussion of prophecies made by their husbands. In 1 Timothy 2:12–14 we also have a prohibition of unqualified and ungifted women usurping authority by taking part in teaching. Paul's strong stress on order and the avoidance of causing offence probably meant in practice that the women of the church sometimes would have to subordinate their own rights to the well-being of the whole church, just as all the church members had to do. However, there is nothing in Paul's letters to necessitate the conclusion that he saw the place of women in worship as intrinsically different from that of men. Rather there is much to indicate that the liberty and equality 'in Christ' of Jew and Greek, of slave and free and of male and female, was fully expressed when the church met together to worship God.

It may be helpful to bring in at this stage another general problem that would arise if one wanted to argue for an interpretation of Paul's words which would support differing practices for men and women in worship. This is in connection with our relationship to God. The more the distinction between the sexes is stressed, the greater the tendency to assume that men relate to God in a different way from women. This is accentuated if one starts arguing that man as a male can be a representative of Christ in a way that a woman can never be and the image of God in a way that a woman is not. How then can a woman be identified with Christ? If we stress Christ's maleness rather than his humanity, how can a woman be sure that he can stand as her representative or that the teaching of for example Hebrews 4:14–5:10 referring to Christ as our High Priest, able to identify with us in all our temptations, applies to her? Like the hermeneutical problem mentioned above this has serious spiritual implications, and cannot be lightly set aside.

Leadership

Just as there appear to have been variations in the precise patterns of worship found in the different churches of the New Testament, so also we do not find one universal fixed pattern of leadership. It is possible that the differences that can be seen merely reflect differing stages of development, so that by the time the Pastorals were written, the leadership of the church at Corinth, for example, which appears from the letters to the Corinthians to have been very unstructured, would have in fact mirrored the more formal situation described in the Pastorals. However, there is no evidence that parallel development in that way ever took place and we can only point out that in the New Testament as we have it, different patterns of leadership did exist.

1 Timothy 2:12 ('I permit no woman to teach or have authority

over men') has been used by some as an indication that no woman should ever take up any office that involves leadership of men. 1 Corinthians 14:34 ('They should be subordinate'), and 1 Corinthians 11:3, ('The head of a woman is her husband') are seen as providing support for this view. Thus G. W. Knight concludes that Paul laid down a 'universally normative regulation which prohibits women from teaching the church and from ruling and teaching men in the church'.[200] However, for the following reasons it is suggested that these passages are not in themselves directly relevant to a discussion of the official leadership in the churches.

a) The concept of headship of husband over wife, or man over woman, does not necessarily involve any idea of authority and in any case is never introduced in the context of leadership in the churches.

b) The 'authority' of 1 Timothy 2:12 refers to a particular kind of domineering authority and is specifically related to teaching and not to all forms of authority or leadership. We have shown that this verse is probably not to be taken as a total prohibition of all teaching of men by women.

c) Teaching in the New Testament was not directly linked to any office or particular group of leaders.[201]

Thus Hommes' conclusion that 'the traditional use of 1 Timothy 2:11–12 and the like as a veto of an official function for women in the church is therefore illegitimate; because a completely different matter is in discussion there, i.e. the decorum of the married women in the service'[202] appears justified. At the very least, we cannot take these passages and assume that the question of women's leadership is then closed. Rather we must look at what Paul has to say on leadership as such.

In fact, we gain knowledge of the leadership in the New Testament church in two different ways. Firstly, we learn from descriptions of individual people who were leaders; what this teaches us about the leadership of women we will discuss at a later stage.[203] Secondly, we learn from specific teaching on the nature of leadership and on the characteristics required in individual leaders. Most of this specific teaching is located in the Pastoral epistles, with particular offices being mentioned elsewhere only in passing (e.g. Philippians 1:1; Acts 20:17).

However, before we come to discuss these particular offices, it is important to keep in mind that leadership in the New Testament is always seen in terms of service rather than of status. That Jesus' teaching in Luke 22:26 ('Rather let the greatest among you become as the youngest and the leader as one who serves ') is implicit in Paul is shown by the way he uses such terms as *diakonos* 'servant' and *diakonia* 'service' in his discussion of leadership. Schmithals's statement concerning apostles – 'The office of apostle does not bestow upon the bearer any kind of spiritual quality which elevates him above the congregation; he is and remains a member of his congregation'[204] – is equally true of all forms of leadership. Leadership is seen as a gift to the whole congregation for the benefit of the whole congregation. Thus, it is interesting to note that while the members of the congregation are often urged to subject themselves to their leaders,[205] leaders are nowhere exhorted to ensure such subjection to themselves.

In a very real sense, responsibility in the churches was corporate. In writing to the churches Paul wrote to the whole congregation, not just to the leaders. Even in Philippians where bishops and deacons are specifically mentioned, the letter is primarily addressed to 'all the saints'. It was the responsibility of the whole congregation to see that the instructions and exhortations given by Paul in his letter were followed. 1 Corinthians 5:4–5, 11 makes it clear that Paul saw discipline in the church as the responsibility of the whole church (cf 2 Thessalonians 3:6; Romans 16:17). The particular leadership of individuals must not be seen as taking away from this corporate responsibility. As far as this kind of corporate leadership was concerned, it was shared by men and women alike as equally members of the congregation.

It is also important to note that we have in fact very little information about the precise relation between 'office' and 'function' in the New Testament church. The Pastoral Epistles make explicit what is apparent elsewhere, that there were those who were appointed to a specific office. However, while we learn much about the characteristics required in those who aspire to office we are told very little about the particular responsibilities and tasks assigned to the holder of any individual office. For example, some, but not all, elders laboured in preaching and teaching (1 Timothy 5:17) and certainly not all preachers and teachers were elders (cf Colossians 3:16; 1 Corinthians 14:26 etc). Daniélou sees the functions of 'ordained ministry' in the New Testament as 'presiding in the congregation, teaching authoritatively and offering the Eucharist'.[206] Later evidence about the activities of ministers in the early church makes this a distinct possibility, but it is not something that can be deduced from the New Testament itself. In fact in the New Testament, there is no clear distinction made between regulated offices and unregulated ministry by those with no official position, beyond what Schweizer calls 'the purely practical need of division'.[207]

Five basic offices have been identified in the New Testament church; apostle, bishop, elder, deacon and widow, although none of these is a precise technical term and there is variety in the use of the terms. Paul tells us nothing at all of the appointment of apostles, although it is clear that he uses the term to refer to others than the Twelve.[208] There has been some debate as to what distinction, if any, can be made between bishops and elders. Some are of the opinion that they are alternative descriptions of the same office, others think that they can be distinguished.[209] A. E. Harvey suggests that the *presbuteroi*[210] were in fact so called because, at least to start with, they were simply the older men in the congregation who would naturally take the lead. He argues that there is no evidence of a similarity between Christian elders and the Jewish elders of the synagogue, and that 'deprived of the Jewish analogy, we have not a scrap of evidence from the early period that the Christian elders were ever organized into anything formal or official, or that they were ever sitting in committee in such a way that they would need a chairman.'[211]

Whatever was the function of elders or of bishops in the New Testament, and whatever was the relationship between them, it is taken for granted that they will be men,[212] and that bishops at least will be older married men with children (1 Timothy 3:2–4; Titus 1:6). Paul's own marital status and the teaching he gives in 1 Corinthians 7 make it likely that he was assuming that in the situation as it was, bishops would be married with children, rather than insisting that they should be. Thus it is better to see 'a bishop must be . . . the husband of one wife' as 'if he is married, he must have only one wife' than as 'he must be married' and similarly it is better to see 'he must . . . keep his children submissive' as 'if he has children, they must be submissive' than as 'he must have children'. It is possible also that he is assuming they will be male rather than insisting that they should be. None of these assumptions is phrased in the form of a command and no theological reasons are given to support any of them.

While Paul apparently takes it for granted that bishops will be male, deacons can be either male or female. There is some disagreement as to whether 'the women' in 1 Timothy 3:11 refers to women deacons or to the wives of male deacons.[213] The fact that the reference is so brief and that male deacons are mentioned both before and after the reference to the women, makes the latter a possibility but the likelihood of the former being correct appears strong. The 'likewise' of verse 11 is parallel to verse 8 where a new class of officials is being introduced, so it seems logical to assume that we are talking about officials in verse 11 also. A single verb co-ordinates the bishops, the deacons and the women, showing that there is some connection quite clearly envisaged between all three. There is no article or possessive pronoun to indicate that we should translate as 'their wives'. There is no reference to the wives of the bishops and surely if particular characteristics were necessary for the wives of deacons it would be necessary for the wives of bishops also to be found worthy of the role. The characteristics required are very similar for both men and women and we know from elsewhere that women deacons did exist.[214] Thus, while we do not know what were the precise responsibilities of deacons, in so far as they belonged to the official leadership of the church, women, in spite of their lack of status in society generally, had a part to play within that leadership. However, again it must be stressed that leadership, whether male or female, was seen primarily in terms of service rather than of authority. The fact that women deacons are specifically mentioned lends support to the view that, at this stage at least, Paul did not envisage the possibility of women bishops.

1 Timothy 5:9–10 mentions a list of widows, which some have seen as referring to a specific order, appointed for ministry within the church. However, although verse 10, 'She must be well attested for her good deeds, as one who has brought up children, shown hospitality, washed the feet of the saints, relieved the afflicted and devoted herself to doing good in every way', has sometimes been seen as a list of duties which were to be carried out by those belonging to such an order, in fact it describes the activities of widows before they could be enrolled, not after. So, while it is quite possible that 'an officially recognized order of widows with definite duties . . . and definite conditions of entry'[215] did exist, it is unlikely that this is what is being described here. In this passage it seems more likely that there is no break after verses 4–8 which deal with provision being made for widows by their families, so that in verses 9–10 Paul goes on to talk about the provision which should be made by the church for those widows with no families. Thus we cannot assume that any separate and distinctively female order of ministry existed in the New Testament.

It appears clear, then, that the leadership of the churches in the New Testament was rather more fluid and unstructured than at first one might assume. If we are to see the precise pattern of leadership found in the New Testament church as normative for all time, then it can be said that the New Testament teaches that senior leaders are always to be male. If, however, McGlashan[216] is right in feeling that the lack of a single system in the New Testament means that we cannot see the pattern of church order found there as a norm, but rather in terms of principles and guidelines, then it will depend on whether the maleness of the bishops is seen as a principle or not. We would suggest that the New Testament does not give a clear indication that it should be seen in that way.

Insofar as leadership was a corporate function of the church, as far as Paul was concerned, women were to play their part alongside the men. Insofar as leadership was individual, those who exercised oversight were normally older men; although this appears to reflect the situation of the time and no theological reason is given for it. Women took part in the leadership of the church as deacons. Because we have no way of knowing what particular roles or functions were associated with which office – if indeed we can see the offices as structured enough to be assigned precise roles – Banks' conclusion that 'there do not seem to be legitimate reasons for ascribing any family, public or church role exclusively to one sex or the other,'[217] appears valid. However, to see sex as not directly relevant to the assigning of tasks within the church does not imply that it is irrelevant to the carrying out of those tasks. Just as a man remains a man, and lives, worships and also leads as a man, so a woman remains a woman and lives, worships and leads as a woman.

5. PAUL: WOMAN IN RELATION TO MAN (II)

Paul's teaching in Romans 5 and in 1 Corinthians 15:22 ('As in Adam all die, so also in Christ shall all be made alive') makes it clear that he saw a very real unity of the human race, both male and female, whether they are 'in Adam' or 'in Christ'. However, alongside that unity (and by no means negating it) there is also diversity, 'for man was not made from woman but woman from man' (1 Corinthians 11:8). Again alongside this, and in a sense bringing the two sexes back together, is the concept of complementarity, 'woman is not independent of man, nor man of woman' (1 Corinthians 11:11). This picture found in Paul of the unity, diversity and complementarity of the sexes, closely reflects the picture we find in Genesis.

Those who see in Genesis a 'creation order' between men and women that is by nature hierarchical, that involves the authority of men over women and that results in certain patterns of behaviour being considered appropriate to a particular sex[218], feel that because he quotes Genesis, Paul is maintaining also that the relation between men and women is essentially hierarchical. Paul's use of such terms as 'head' and 'submission' is seen as providing support for this view. However, we have shown[219] that sexual hierarchy is not self-evidently taught by the Genesis creation narratives, but rather has to be read into the text. The fact that Paul quotes from Genesis therefore does not necessarily mean that he saw a hierarchical order between the sexes. Similarly, we have shown[220] that it is not valid to see the use of 'head' and 'submission' as automatically indicating such a hierarchy. It is interesting that in 1 Corinthians 11:8–9 Paul quotes from Genesis 2:21–23 in order to stress the distinction between the sexes and in particular the fact that the woman gives herself for the man, whereas in Ephesians 5:31 he quotes Genesis 2:24 in the context of stressing the husband giving himself for his wife.

However, while neither in Genesis nor in Paul is there any teaching that necessitates the relation between the sexes being seen in terms of hierarchy, nevertheless Paul restresses that there is a diversity between the sexes and that there is order in the relationship. D. S. Bailey describes sexual order as 'the general form of relation subsisting ontologically between male and female as personal constituents of the dual being Man. Like sex itself this order is essentially a mystery.' While it cannot be defined, this order 'remains intrinsically an order of mutual complementarity, wherein neither sex is subordinate or superordinate to the other'.[221]

In Paul's thought, the unity and diversity between the sexes resulting in their complementarity is seen particularly clearly in the marriage relation, although 1 Corinthians 11 indicates that he sees it in a wider context than just in marriage. However, while Paul speaks often of the marriage relation he does not elaborate on the working out of the relationship between members of different sexes as such, outside marriage. Perhaps his instructions to Timothy, 'Treat... older women like mothers, younger women like sisters' (1 Timothy 5:2), can be seen in this light, but there is very little else.

Thus while Paul says much about the behaviour of different groups within the church, including the different sexes, there is very little explicit teaching given as to how the sexes should relate to each other. It is possible that the extent to which women shared with Paul as co-workers is an indication of how he felt the complementarity between the sexes should be worked out within the church community. Apart from this indication we are simply left with the fact of and the necessity for maintaining both the unity and the diversity between the sexes while also acknowledging and working out their complementarity. Bailey describes this as the necessity of both 'the preservation of sexual integrity and the acceptance of sexual partnership'.[222] Maybe the lack of teaching on how this should be worked out in practice and the emphasis

Paul places on the giving of a good impression to outsiders means that the precise application of Paul's teaching will vary with differing cultures. Perhaps Paul's conclusion to his discussion of the marriage relation and the relation between Christ and the church applies here too. 'This is a great mystery.'

6. PAUL: THE RELATION OF CHRISTIAN WOMEN TO THOSE OUTSIDE THE CHRISTIAN COMMUNITY

Paul was very concerned that Christians should always behave in such a way that outsiders would be given no opportunity to criticize them. This is particularly important for their attitude towards the ruling authorities and their behaviour in society generally, but even their behaviour towards those of their own family and towards other members of the Christian community is to some extent to be regulated by the impression that would be given to those outside.[223] The principle underlying their behaviour is that it should always be glorifying to God and that it should bring no discredit on the gospel they proclaimed.

This principle applied to slave and free, to young and old and to male and female without differentiation. Much of the behaviour and characteristics required of different groups was the same, as is indicated by the fact that they are often addressed as a whole, and by the repeated use of the term 'likewise' (e.g. 1 Timothy 3:11; Titus 2:3–6). However in certain cases the behaviour considered appropriate to each will vary, and Paul does sometimes speak to each group separately.

As far as the women were concerned, they were to 'love their husbands and children, to be sensible, chaste, domestic, kind and submissive to their husbands' (Titus 2:4–5). They were to dress modestly (1 Timothy 2:9), and to devote themselves to 'doing good in every way'. This principle of behaving in a way which was beyond reproach would often necessitate going the 'extra mile'. Thus, for example, while Paul never calls on a wife to be 'obedient' to her husband, in the cultural situation of many of the churches to which he wrote this would have been generally expected, and therefore would be the appropriate behaviour for a wife, particularly if her husband was not a Christian.

Paul proclaimed the liberty and equality of all who were 'in Christ', but although these principles were implicit in all he said and would automatically lead to changes in the attitudes and behaviour of those within the church, he never calls directly for an overturn of the order of society outside the church. Christians must live and work within that society. Thus, like all Christians, women were to relate to and behave in the society in which they lived in such a way that they would 'adorn the doctrine of God our Saviour' (Titus 2:10) within that society. Perhaps if this was done, it was inevitable that the society too would change.

7. OTHER NEW TESTAMENT DOCTRINAL TEACHING

In the rest of the New Testament, there are only two passages which are concerned specifically with the relation between men and women or with the place of women as opposed to men. Both of these (Hebrews 13:4 and 1 Peter 3:1–7) are concerned with marriage. Outside these, and in fact also within them, there is, as in Paul's writings, the implicit assumption that the church is made up of both men and women who are equally children of God. Thus, the 'chosen race, a royal priesthood, a holy nation, God's own people,' consisting of all who are 'chosen and destined by God the Father and sanctified by the Spirit for obedience to Jesus Christ and for sprinkling with his blood' (1 Peter 2:9, 1:2), involves both slave and free, both male and female.

Hebrews 13:4

'Let marriage be held in honour among all, and let the marriage bed be undefiled, for God will judge the immoral and adulterous.' This verse reiterates Paul's teaching on marriage by insisting that it should be 'held in honour among all'. The second half of the verse indicates that the way in which marriage might be dishonoured is seen primarily in terms of immorality and unfaithfulness. However, it is possible that the reference here is also to those who would dishonour marriage by teaching that celibacy or sexual asceticism is to be more highly valued. This verse takes for granted the fact that marriage is ordained by God and that it is a unique and exclusive relationship. The marriage covenant is never to be treated lightly, either by the partners involved or by those outside; God himself will act against those who break such a covenant.

1 Peter 3:1–7

This passage forms part of a section (2:11 – 3:17) in which Peter describes the behaviour, and in particular the subjection, that is required from those who are Christian believers. There are two basic principles that should govern their conduct. Firstly, 'The individual's awareness that God's eye is upon him, and his sense of what is valued in God's sight, should determine how he acts.'[224] Secondly, his behaviour should be influenced by 'a sensitiveness to the effect of Christian conduct on public opinion'.[225] Peter, again like Paul, was concerned with the impression that the world outside would gain of Christ through their observation of the lives of Christ's people. Chapter 2:11–17 and 3:8–17 speak of how these principles should be worked out in the lives of all Christians, chapter 2:18–25 applies them specifically to household slaves and chapter 3:1–7 specifically to wives and husbands.

There has been some speculation as to the reason why six verses are devoted to the behaviour of wives and only one to husbands. The reason is unlikely to be the fact that women were more numerous in the early churches [226] (the evidence that this was so is in any case not particularly strong as far as the very early years are concerned). Rather, wives had legally much less freedom than their husbands, and this left particular problems for the Christian wife of a non-Christian husband;[227] problems which would not apply in the reverse situation of a Christian husband with a non-Christian wife.

1 Peter 3:1 'Likewise, you wives, be submissive to your husbands, so that some, though they do not obey the word, may be won without a word by the behaviour of their wives.'

The 'likewise' here links back to both verse 13 and verse 18, so that there is some similarity between the submissive attitude required from citizens to the state, from servants to masters and from wives to husbands. The 'your' (*idiois*, more properly 'your own') makes it clear that Peter is speaking specifically of the husband and wife relationship and not of the man/woman relation generally. Selwyn feels that this word (i.e. *idiois*) 'delivers the passage from any charge of inculcating the "inferiority" of women to men and shows that the subordination is one of function within the intimate circle of the home.'[228] However, the 'be submissive' does not in any case imply any inferiority as such, and it may be better to speak here of the submissive attitude required of the wife rather than of any subordinate function. Certainly, at the time wives were considered to exercise a subordinate function and maybe accepting that this was so was a part of the submission required of them; but the emphasis here and right through to verse 6 is on attitude and demeanour rather than on function as such. In any event, Selwyn's point holds. It is illegitimate to use this passage as evidence that there is a general requirement of submission from all women to all men for Peter speaks here solely within the context of marriage.

Because Peter mentions the possibility of 'some' being won, it is not clear whether he is calling for submission as a basic requirement from all wives to their husbands, with the conversion of 'some' non-Christian husbands being a desirable side-effect of this, or whether the whole verse speaks only of marriages where the husband is not a Christian. In Ephesians 5:22, Paul shows that submission is the proper attitude for every Christian wife and it is probable that Peter too is taking this for granted. However, it does seem that in this instance Peter's primary concern is for those whose husbands are not believers. All Christians were to behave in such a way as to give the best possible impression to outsiders. An ideal wife of the time would accept without question her husband's religion.[229] However, for a Christian wife to renounce her faith was impossible, as to do so would be to go directly against the will of God. It was very important, therefore, that she take special care to act as the ideal wife in every other way.

1 Peter 3:2–6 '...when they see your reverent and chaste behaviour. Let not yours be the outward adorning with braiding of hair, decoration of gold, and wearing of robes, but let it be the hidden person of the heart with the imperishable jewel of a gentle and quiet spirit, which in God's sight is very precious. So once the holy women who hoped in God used to adorn themselves and were submissive to their husbands, as Sarah obeyed Abraham, calling him lord. And you are now her children if you do right and let nothing terrify you.'

These verses expand on the behaviour and bearing seen as ideal for a wife. She is to attract her husband to Christ by her pure and reverent behaviour. She is not to use 'coquettrie féminine'[230] in her hairstyle, jewels and clothes, but rather to cultivate and express 'a calm and imperturbable spirit, placid and gentle, in relation to both people and circumstances'.[231] It is important to note that while Peter is speaking here particularly to wives, the characteristics he mentions cannot be seen as especially appropriate to women as such; for 'the chaste bearing of the Christian wife is intimately bound up with those instincts of reverence which are an essential ingredient of the Christian life in general.'[232] One cannot help feeling that in calling on the Christian wives to have 'a gentle and quiet spirit' (v 4) Peter had in mind the words of Jesus, 'Learn from me, for I am gentle and lowly in heart' (Matthew 11:29). The Christlike life is intrinsically attractive and Peter wants these wives to remember that in all their dealings with their non-Christian husbands. Sarah, in her attitude to Abraham, can stand as an example to them. They are to do what is right, that is presumably, to live as God would have them live in this situation and not to be terrified by the difficult position in which they find themselves.

In verse 6, the use of the aorist *hupēkousen*, 'obeyed', would seem to indicate one particular act of obedience. However, the only occasion in Scripture where Sarah is recorded as calling Abraham 'lord' is in Genesis 18:12, when no obedience or submission is involved. It seems likely that Peter here is reiterating Jewish tradition which idealized Sarah, rather than quoting from Genesis.[233] Chrysostom, commenting on this passage and linking it with Genesis 21:10, where God tells Abraham to obey Sarah, says 'Well, this is what I want to point out, that both he obeyed her in all things and she him.'[234]

1 Peter 3:7 'Likewise, you husbands, live considerately (*kata gnōsin*, literally, 'according to knowledge') with your wives, bestowing honour on the woman as the weaker sex, since you are joint heirs of the grace of life, in order that your prayers may not be hindered.'

Selwyn believes that the 'likewise' here is either just a connecting word not showing a particular link with the previous verses, or else he sees the link in terms of 'a foundation of love' that underlies all these instructions.[235] However, there seems to be no reason to ignore the parallel in 3:1, where the reference is to the submissiveness referred to in 2:13 and 2:18. If this is so, then verse 7 must also be seen in the whole context of the submission of one to another.

There have been many interpretations of the fact that a man must live with his wife 'according to knowledge'.

i. The RSV, 'live considerately', itself an interpretation, is taken up by Best (p.127) and expanded as 'not considering his rights and privileges, but his duties'. The knowledge referred to is thus knowledge of what is right.

ii. Similar to this is Kelly's view (p.132) that this knowledge is 'Christian insight and tact, a conscience sensitive to God's will'.

iii. Stibbs is of the opinion that the knowledge in question is knowledge of the wife, that is, the husband must have 'a proper awareness of her condition in relation to himself, both in nature and grace' (p.127).

iv. Stendahl also sees the knowledge as of the wife, but particularly of the fact that the wife is the weaker vessel. (*The Bible and the Role of Women* p.31.)

v. A rather different view is that of W. Beare who states that 'Certainly the knowledge of God is meant... The relationship of God determines the nature of the marriage relationship' (p.131 cf Kee and Young p.443).

It is by no means clear which of these aspects – knowledge of what constitutes right behaviour, knowledge of the wife's position or knowledge of God – is really being emphasized here by Peter. Perhaps there is an element of truth in all of them. However, whatever the knowledge refers to, it is such as will lead husbands to bestow honour on their wives.

There are two factors which influence this honour. Firstly, the fact that the wives are 'weaker vessels' and secondly, that they are 'joint-heirs'. The weakness referred to here could be physical, intellectual or moral. If the latter is meant, then 'we should have to see in it a vestige of the low estimation of the moral stamina of women, common to Jews and Greeks.'[236] It seems more likely that the reference is to physical strength, so that the husband should 'recognize her more limited physical powers and give her corresponding consideration and protection.'[237] It is also possible that what Peter means is the legal weakness of the wife in relation to her husband. If this is so, then he is saying that although the husband was in a stronger position, legally, he was not to abuse this, but was to honour his wife, remembering her equal status with him before God. Thus a Christian husband was to regard his wife not in terms of her legal position, which was undoubtedly weaker than his, but rather in terms of her spiritual position, which was not.

It is important to note that in speaking of her husband and wife as 'joint-heirs', Peter is according to the woman 'full religious equality with man – a thought impossible for Judaism'.[238] That is, Peter, just as Paul does, reiterates the radical concepts introduced by Jesus. Spicq thinks that the reference to joint-heirs means that there is 'une affinité particulière',[239] a special link, between husbands and wives which is something extra to the common heritage of all Christians. However, this seems to be reading into the text a little more than it will bear. Peter is simply pointing out that before God, man and wife stand in exactly the same position and that this common inheritance will affect the way in which they relate to each other on all levels.

In the final phrase of the verse, 'the underlying principle is that a man's relation to God is not independent of his relation to his fellows.'[240] This is particularly true in the close relation between husband and wife. The 'your' is plural, and it seems more likely that it is the prayers of both that might be affected, rather than simply the prayers of the husband alone. If a couple fail to recognize or act upon the implications of their being 'joint-heirs of the grace of life', then their relationship with God, expressed in prayer, will be seriously hindered.

Thus, while Peter recognizes and accepts the cultural and social situation as it is, and gives advice for living within that situation, nevertheless, he too gives us a remarkably egalitarian picture. It must not be forgotten how unusual it was for husbands and wives both to be addressed. Moreover Peter applies the same principles to the behaviour of both husband and wife even though these principles may lead to different behaviour patterns in any given cultural situation. He in no way obscures the distinction between the sexes, quite the reverse, but he does make explicit their spiritual equality.

5

Acts and Epistles:
Community Practice

We learn much from the Acts about the founding of the various churches and much from the epistles about the problems which beset those churches and about the way in which the writers felt that those problems should be dealt with. However, we have in fact, very little detailed information about the way in which members of the Christian community in New Testament times lived out their daily lives. This is particularly true of the way in which the relation between the sexes was worked out in the life of the church. The fact that most of the information we do have is gained from passing references or from greetings means that we must beware of any presentation of a generalized picture. Nevertheless, we can obtain from this information valuable insights into the place of women in the New Testament church.

1. MARRIAGE

Paul and Peter are both greatly concerned with the relationship between married couples, with preserving the sanctity of marriage and with the maintenance of Christian family life, and it seems certain that most of the Christians would have been married. However, apart from knowing that 'the other apostles and the brothers of the Lord and Cephas' were all married and that their wives accompanied them on their travelling ministry (1 Corinthians 9:5), we know for certain of only two other married couples. It is possible that others mentioned together, such as Philemon and Apphia (Philemon 1:2), or Andronicus and Junia[1] (Romans 16:7), were in fact married couples but only Ananias and Sapphira, and Priscilla and Aquila are definitely described as such.

Of the former we know only the rather sad story of the incident which led to their deaths (Acts 5:1–11). Two things are apparent from this story. Firstly they had acted together in the matter, coming to a joint decision to deceive the church about how much they were giving, and secondly that in spite of this each was individually responsible. Like Ananias, Sapphira was accountable for her own sin and no necessity for submitting to the wishes of her husband could be used as an excuse for avoiding her personal responsibility.

Of Priscilla and Aquila we know much more. They are mentioned six times, always together.[2] We know that they were Jews who travelled together widely in the Roman Empire, whether on business trips, because of the Roman Emperor's directive that all Jews should leave Rome, or as part of Paul's party of missionaries. They worked together as tent-makers. Together they helped and instructed the eloquent teacher Apollos. Together they led a house church. They are described as fellow-workers with Paul and at some stage they risked their lives for his sake. Clearly they were influential in the building up of several of the churches.

In four of the six references to them, Priscilla (Paul preferred to use Prisca, the proper form of the name, whereas Luke uses the diminutive Priscilla) is named first. We cannot be certain of the significance of this fact.[3] It could mean that Priscilla came from a much more important family or it may imply that she was more active and perhaps more influential in the work of the church.[4] It is certainly clear that Priscilla was at least as active as her husband and there is not the slightest hint of anything other than an equal partnership in every aspect of their relationship. Maybe Paul, who knew and loved this couple well, had their marriage in mind when he wrote his lovely description of the marriage relationship in Ephesians 5.

This couple were undoubtedly remarkable, not the least in their much travelling; and this fact means that they cannot necessarily be seen as typical. Nor is there any real reason why their marriage should stand as a pattern for all Christian couples; however, it is perhaps of some significance that theirs is the only marriage of which the New Testament gives any real detail.

2. OFFICIAL MINISTRIES

We have discussed the difficulty involved in maintaining a precise distinction between official ministries in the New Testa-

ment churches.⁵ This difficulty is heightened because, while there
are many general references to the different forms of official
ministry, there are only a very small number of occasions when
particular individuals, either men or women, are described as
holders of a specific office.

Apostles

Apart from the references to the Twelve as apostles found in
Acts, the only undisputed references to particular apostles are to
Paul himself (Romans 1:1; 1 Corinthians 9:1, etc.), and to Peter
(Galatians 1:18–19). It is probable that Barnabas (1 Corinthians
9:6; Acts 14:4–14), James (Galatians 1:19), Andronicus and Junia
(Romans 16:7) are also described as apostles. With reference to
Andronicus and Junia, it is generally agreed that 'notable in the
ranks of the apostles' is 'a much more probable rendering' of
episēmoi en tois apostolois than 'well known to the apostles',⁶
although there are some scholars who prefer the latter.⁷ It is quite
possible that 'Junia' refers to a female, although we cannot be
absolutely certain either way. *Iounian* could be a fairly common
female name, or it could be a shortened form of a somewhat less
common male name. It is impossible to decide which it is in this
case.⁸ Goguel is right in his statement that 'a bare possibility is not
sufficient to permit us to say that the title apostle was borne by a
woman'⁹, but nevertheless the possibility must be noted.
Chrysostom, writing in the fourth century was clearly convinced
that the reference here does indicate that Andronicus and Junia
were apostles and that Junia was a woman. He writes, 'Oh how
great is the devotion of this woman that she should be counted
worthy of the appellation of apostle.'¹⁰

Elders and bishops

There is no woman anywhere in the New Testament who is ever
described as being either an elder or a bishop. However, one
should also note that no man is ever described as being a bishop
and the only men who are specifically referred to as elders are Peter
(1 Peter 5:1) and the writer of 2 and 3 John, both of whom refer to
themselves in this way. It does seem likely that bishops and elders,
if the two can be distinguished, were almost invariably men.
However, the fact that five out of the six passages which mention
house churches refer to women among the leaders,¹¹ and the

possibility that the 'elect lady' of 2 John 1 is in fact an individual leader of the church,[12] mean that we cannot be absolute in our assumption that these positions were never held by women.

Deacons

It is difficult to decide when, if ever, the term *diakonos* refers to a definite office and when it is simply being used as a general term for servant. The noun is directly applied to only five individuals: Paul (Ephesians 3:7; Colossians 1:23), Tychicus (Ephesians 6:21; Colossians 4:7), Epaphras (Colossians 1:7) and Timothy (1 Thessalonians 3:2; 1 Timothy 4:6), who were all men, and Phoebe (Romans 16:1) who was a woman. As far as Phoebe is concerned, Murray suggests that 'there is neither need nor warrant to suppose that she occupied or exercised what amounted to an ecclesiastical office comparable to that of the diaconate.'[13] However, in Phoebe's case in particular, if the word does not describe an office it is very difficult to see why *diakonos*, which is a specifically masculine term, was used rather than some feminine alternative describing service generally.

1 Timothy 3:11 does provide support for the diaconate consisting of both men and women.[14] Leenhardt does not accept that 1 Timothy 3:11 refers to women deacons, but nevertheless of Romans 16:1 he says, 'It is admitted that here *diakonos* designates an office, an established function, having *ousan* as a participle and *ekklēsias* as its genitive.'[15] The lack of any feminine equivalent for *diakonos* makes it likely that there was no distinction seen between the office of male and female deacons. Phoebe was a deacon, not a deaconess having completely distinct duties.

Romans 16:2 lends support to the view that Phoebe exercised some kind of official ministry, although we can only speculate as to the particular duties that this ministry entailed.[16] The Roman Christians are to give Phoebe all the assistance she required, for she had been a 'helper' (*prostatis*) of many, including Paul. It is possible that this help was simply 'a matter of material and administrative assistance'[17], but if so it is difficult to envisage why the church at Rome was asked to help her in her work. The word *prostatis* when used technically denotes 'the legal representative of strangers, ...for as aliens they were deprived of civil rights.' Leenhardt suggests that perhaps 'Phoebe had had occasion to intervene on behalf of Christians and at times before authority.'[18] However, Paul, as a Roman citizen, would not have required help of this kind, and in fact the word is very often used in a nontechnical sense. Banks sees it as significant that 'the cognate terms from the same root are used elsewhere to describe the activities of those who exercise leadership in the churches.'[19]

On the basis of the use of *diakonos* elsewhere, Ellis considers that Phoebe must have been engaged in 'preaching and teaching' at Cenchrae. [20] This conclusion may not be quite warranted, but there is certainly no reason to suppose that the help and service given by Phoebe as a *diakonos*, as that of Paul, Tychicus, Epaphras and Timothy, did not involve spiritual as well as material responsibilities.

Teachers

There appears to have been no official teaching office as such, but we are told that Priscilla taught the great orator Apollos (Acts 18:26) and in spite of 1 Timothy 2:12 there is no indication that this was in any way seen as wrong.

3. IN THE GENERAL LIFE OF THE CHURCHES

The Church at Jerusalem

It may be correct to say that the church proper was founded on the Day of Pentecost, but the nucleus of this primitive church was already in existence. This nucleus consisted not merely of the remaining eleven disciples, but 'in one accord, leading with them a life devoted to prayer, there were also "the women"'[21] as well as Jesus' mother and brothers. There appears to have been no difficulty here about the women praying alongside the men. Acts 2 shows that women shared fully and equally in the experience of Pentecost, so that in this act of giving his Spirit by which God founded his church both men and women were involved (Acts 2:1–4, 17–18). The group of new converts consisted equally of men and women with no distinction made between them. In Acts 2:41, for example, we are told that about three thousand people were baptized, with no indication as to the proportion of men and women; this is a change from the more usual method of counting only the men (cf Luke 19:14).

Acts presents the twelve apostles[22] as the clear leaders of the Jerusalem church in the early stages, to be succeeded later apparently by James the brother of the Lord. However the mention by name of 'Mary, the mother of John, whose other name was

Mark', in whose home they met, indicates that others did have their own part to play. It was the Twelve, for example, who recognized the necessity for appointing men to oversee the distribution to the widows, but Acts 6:5 shows that it was the whole community, consisting of both men and women, who made the decision to accept the apostles' suggestion and who selected the seven men who were appointed.

Thus, while there is every indication that leadership roles within the Jerusalem community were held largely, if not entirely, by men, nevertheless women were accepted fully into the membership of the church from the beginning in a way unknown in Judaism. They shared in the prayer, in prophecy and in the decision making activity of the church.

The Church at Rome

We know nothing of the founding of the church at Rome and very little of its life, but Romans 16 gives us some insight into its composition.[23] We learn that while they are addressed as one church, they also met in smaller groups (vv 4, 14, 15), that some of the members had travelled to Rome from elsewhere (vv 3, 5), and that there were several families amongst the believers (vv 10, 11, 13, 15). Of the twenty-six people who are mentioned by name, six, or if we include Junia as a woman,[24] seven are women. However, of the eleven who are given a specific designation rather than simply being greeted or described as beloved, five are definitely women and five men, with the eleventh being Junia. We have already spoken of Priscilla, Aquila, Andronicus and Junia. Of the remaining men, Urbanus is described as a fellow-worker (*sunergon*), Apelles as approved (*dokimon*) in Christ, and Rufus as eminent (*eklekton*) in the Lord. Of the women, Mary and Persis are both described as having worked hard (*polla ekopiasen*) and Tryphaena and Tryphosa as being workers (*kopiōsas*) in the Lord.

We cannot be sure of the precise implications of these terms, and Goguel's warning that there may be a 'rhetorical factor at work', for 'somewhat exaggerated terms were used loosely in letters of recommendation'[25], must be kept in mind, although to describe people as 'workers' does not seem particularly effusive. There is certainly no reason why we should interpret words when applied to women in a different way from when they are applied to men, and as Daniélou points out, these terms generally refer to a 'participation in the work of evangelism', and 'the expression "to work in the Lord" can only refer to apostolic tasks.'[26] It is perhaps significant that in 1 Corinthians 16:16 Paul uses the same words that are applied here and elsewhere to women, when he instructs the church at Corinth to 'be subject to... every fellow worker and labourer'. Certainly the impression is given in Romans 16 that women shared equally with men in the life and the leadership of the church at Rome.

The Church at Philippi

This church was founded when Paul, in spite of his Jewish background, went to a group of women, unqualified to start a synagogue, and preached, 'obviously in... the expectation that from them might be drawn the nucleus of a Christian cell which in turn would develop into the church at Philippi'[27], Lydia, a business woman from Thyatira, was the first convert. The church began to meet in her house, and it is extremely likely that she would, in the early stages at least, have been its leader. The first believers were women, but it is likely that there were men among Lydia's household, who were baptized and who would naturally look to Lydia for leadership. They were soon joined by others, including the local gaoler and his household.

In the epistle to the Philippians, 'not only is there no hint of any restriction on women, but on the contrary, it shows the Philippian church to be one in which women played a prominent part.'[28] Of the four people mentioned by name in the epistle as being workers, two are men and two women. Epaphroditus, 'my brother and fellow-worker' had been sent to Paul by the church at Philippi with a gift from the church. Euodia, Syntyche, and Clement were all those who had 'laboured side by side with me in the gospel ... with ... the rest of my fellow-workers' (4:3).

Blum[29] considers that this description in 4:3 cannot refer to an official ministry, because the verb to labour when used to describe official ministry normally needs a special qualification as in 1 Timothy 5:17 where certain of the elders 'labour in preaching and teaching'. However, there is no reason why 'in the gospel' cannot be seen as a sufficient qualification here. Goguel acknowledges that this verse does prove that Euodia and Syntyche had themselves played an active part in the preaching of the gospel, but does not accept that this implies that all women could or did play such a part.[30] Yet Paul does not criticize these two for their work, rather he 'accepts their prominence and influential position in the church as well as their right to express themselves'.[31] He criticizes only their conflict. We cannot be certain of the exact nature of their labour, although the term is too strong to be applied to mere material assistance, but we do know that these women had 'contended with the Apostle in the cause of the Gospel and had gained a position of such influence as to make their present conflict a risk to the well-being of the church.'[32] We know also that there is no indication whatsoever of any difference either in status or in function between men and women in the church at Philippi.

In the Other Churches

Of the constitution of the other churches we know less. In Thessalonica for example, we know that 'some Jews, a great many of the devout Greeks and not a few of the leading women' (Acts 17:4) became Christians, but we know very little else. At Colossae we know only that a group met in the house of Nympha (Colossians 4:15) and another in the house of Philemon (Philemon 1–2), that Epaphras was a worker sent out from the church (Colossians 4:12) and that Archippus had some sort of a 'ministry' (4:17). At Corinth we know that women played a major role, and we have discussed elsewhere the way in which Paul dealt with the problems they had in sorting out what was the proper way of expressing their sexual identity and the relation between the sexes. At Cenchreae Phoebe worked in the church as a deacon, and at Caesarea the four un-married daughters of Philip were all prophets. In fact, in almost every church of which we have details, women were prominent among the nucleus of believers and often played a definite part in leadership.

Community Practice: Conclusion

We would feel that the evidence does not support the conclusion of Blum that 'the examination of all the references in the Pauline epistles and in Acts...shows that women definitely played an active part...without however exercising a missionary or teaching office of any kind'.[33] If we are to remove any missionary or teaching content, and any implication of official leadership from the terms applied in the New Testament to women, then we must do so also when these terms are applied to men; this would leave us with almost nothing to say about leadership in the churches as the same terminology is used with reference to both men and women.

The impression is gained from both Acts and the epistles that the leaders and in particular the senior leaders in the churches were far more often male than female. However, women, in some cases, clearly did play a major role in leadership. There is no indication that leadership when it was exercised by women, was in any sense different from that exercised by men. Just as with the part played by men and women in worship, the only differences in the task carried out are those intangible ones that result from the men worshipping and leading as men, and the women as women.

It does appear that a much greater part was played by women in the churches of Macedonia and Rome than in Jerusalem and the more Eastern regions. Banks suggests that this "no doubt reflects the greater freedom enjoyed by women in such areas but it also testifies to the extension by Paul of greater liberty to women where that could be practised without causing scandal, as well as the elevation of women to a place in religious work for which we have no parallel in contemporary practice."[34] The equality of the sexes in their relation to God is thus reflected in the practice of the churches in such a way as possible or appropriate within the cultural context of those churches, but certainly in a much greater way than is sometimes acknowledged.

6

Conclusion

It is apparent that, although in certain cases we have not been given enough information to build up a complete picture of the attitude to women found in biblical times, and in other cases there is enough ambiguity to warn us against coming too dogmatically to firm conclusions, nevertheless we find a remarkable level of both clarity and consistency in the biblical material relating to women.

The Old Testament deals with a male-orientated and male-dominated society, but in spite of this, women, though secondary, are shown to be members of the covenant community with an important role, not only as wives and mothers, but as individuals. First century Judaism, on the other hand, presents women as being subordinate and inferior to men in every sphere, with no real place outside the home, though within the home their role was recognized as important. The Graeco-Roman world, in practice, had an even lower view of women, though there were exceptions.

The attitude of Jesus, seen in all four gospels, contrasts sharply with this background. While he in no way negates the distinction between the sexes, there is very little difference in his approach to males and females. Women, like men, are seen as responsible for their own decisions and capable of spiritual understanding. They are equally free to talk to, follow, be friends with and serve Jesus. The teaching of Jesus that it was possible for men and women to relate to each other in a way other than the specifically sexual, is restressed in the epistles and lived out in the life of the church, which was a community of men and women seeking together to follow the Lord.

The New Testament presents no difference in the way that men and women relate to God or in the way that God relates to them. The relation between men and women is presented in terms of the three principles of diversity, unity, and complementarity. There is diversity in that they were created distinctly and differently and that distinction can and must never be negated; unity in that they are one in Christ and stand side by side as heirs of God, and complementarity in that they are interdependent and each needs the other if their lives are to be lived as God intended them to be. There is a remarkably egalitarian picture of marriage presented; the male is seen as prior in the marriage, but the meaning of this priority is not developed and it does not self-evidently involve authority as such.

In the church, women were accepted as full members of the community. They were seen as individuals in their own right, responsible before God for their own behaviour. No function or activity within the church was specifically or absolutely barred to women: they could, and apparently did, play a full part in the life and worship of the churches. Senior leaders were almost always males, but women could and did exercise leadership within the churches, and where female leadership did exist it appears to be no different in kind from male leadership.

A great emphasis is placed on the importance of glorifying God by giving a good impression to outsiders, so that behaviour sometimes needed to be regulated not only by what was right, although this of course was the primary consideration, but also by what was appropriate in a particular cultural situation. The New Testament only rarely gives a direct call for specific changes in behaviour patterns; thus slavery is never explicitly condemned. However it has become clear that the New Testament teaching regarding the place of women, particularly when seen in the light of its contemporary background, is revolutionary. This teaching, if it had been properly applied, would have brought radical changes both in attitude and in behaviour.

It is my contention that these conclusions, if correct, point to the need for a re-examination of the attitude of the church today. It is not enough simply to look at the churches and reconsider whether or not certain extra jobs or activities should possibly be permitted to women after all. We need a drastic reappraisal of our whole outlook. It is possible that in some ways we have missed out on the way that God wants men and women to work together in the church and to be together as the church; to live out their diversity unity and complementarity. It may be that it is only in modern society that some questions have been able to be raised, but we must make sure that the answers to questions raised in today's society are not dictated by that society – or for that matter by the ideas of a previous society – but reflect a genuine biblical view of Man.

Bibliography

Aalen, S., 'A Rabbinic Formula in 1 Corinthians 14:34' *St.Ev.II* (1964), pp.513–525.

Abbott, J. K., *Ephesians and Colossians* ICC (T. & T. Clark, Edinburgh 1897).

Abbott-Smith, G., *A Manual Greek Lexicon of the N.T.* (T. & T. Clark, Edinburgh 1937).

Albright, W. F. & Mann, C. S., *Matthew* (Anchor Bible, Doubleday, New York 1971).

Anderson, H., *Mark* NCB (Oliphants, London 1976).

Anderson, J. A., *Woman's Warfare and Ministry* (Christian Herald, London 1935).

Aquinas, T., *Summa Theologica* Q93.

Argyle, A. W., *Matthew* (Cambridge Bible Commentary C.U.P. 1963).

Arndt, W. F., *Luke* (Concordia, St. Louis 1956).

Arndt, W. F. & Gingrich, F. W., *A Greek-English Lexicon of the N.T. and Other Early Christian Literature* (Chicago University Press, 1957).

Augustine, *De Trinitatis* 7.10; *De Genesi ad Litteram* 9.5, 8.3.

Bailey, D. S., *The Man-Woman Relation in Christian Thought* (Longman's, London 1959).

Bailey, J. A., 'Initiation and the Primal Woman in Gilgamesh and Genesis 1–3' *JBL* 89 (1970) p.137.

Banks, R., 'Paul and Women's Liberation' *Interchange* 18 (1976), pp.81–105.

Barrett, C. K., *John* (SPCK, London 1955); *Romans* (A. & C. Black, London 1962); *1 Corinthians* (A. & C. Black, London 1971); *The Pastoral Epistles* (Clarendon, Oxford 1963).

Barth, K., *Church Dogmatics* III.1, III.4 (T. & T. Clark, Edinburgh 1961).

Barth, M., *Ephesians* (Anchor Bible Doubleday, New York 1974).

Beare, F. W., *1 Peter* (Blackwell, Oxford 1958).

Beasley-Murray, G. R., *Revelation* (Oliphants, London 1974).

Beckwith, R. T. & Duffield, G. E., 'Towards a Better Solution' *Ch.* 86 (1972), pp.100–112.

Bedale, S., 'The Meaning of *Kephalē* in the Pauline Epistles' *JTS* 5 (1954), p.211.

Best, E., *1 Peter* NCB (Oliphants, London 1971).

Beyer, H. W., 'Diakoneō' *TDNT* II.

Birney, L., *The Role of Women in the New Testament Church* (CBRF, Pinner 1971 reprinted JCBRF 33 (1982)).

Black, M., *Romans* NCB (Oliphants, London 1973).

Bliss, K., *The Service and Status of Women in the Churches* (SCM, London 1952).

Blum, G. G., 'The Office of Women in the New Testament' *Ch.* 85 (1971), pp.175–189.

Boucher, M., 'Some Unexplored Parallels to 1 Corinthians 11:11–12 and Galatians 3:28' *CBQ* 31 (1969), pp.50–58.

Bowman, J., *Mark* (Brill, Leiden 1965).

Brown, C., 'Apostle' *DNTT* I (Paternoster, Exeter 1975), pp.126–137.

Brown, R., 'Roles of Women in the Fourth Gospel' *Th.St.* 36 (1975), pp.688–699.

Bruce, F. F., *New Testament History* (Nelson, London 1969); *Acts* (Tyndale Press, London 1952); *Romans* (Tyndale Press, London 1963); *1 & 2 Corinthians* NCB (Oliphants, London 1971); *Ephesians* (Pickering and Inglis, London 1961).

Brunner, E., *Romans* (Lutterworth, London 1959).

Bultmann, R., *John* (Blackwell, Oxford 1971).

Caird, G. B., 'Paul and Women's Liberty' *BJRL* 34 (1972), pp.268–281; *Principalities and Powers* (Clarendon, Oxford 1956); *Luke* Pelican Commentary (A. & C. Black, London 1963); *Revelation* (A. & C. Black, London 1964)

Calvin, J., *Genesis* (Eerdman's, Grand Rapids 1948); *Harmony of Matthew, Mark & Luke* III (Eerdman's, Grand Rapids 1948); *Corinthians* I (Eerdman's, Grand Rapids 1948); *Pastoral Epistles* (Eerdman's, Grand Rapids 1948).

Cartlidge, D. R., '1 Corinthians 7 as a Foundation for a Christian Sex Ethic' *J of R* 55 (1975), p.220.

Chrysostom, J., *Romans* Vol.11, Library of Nicene and Post-Nicene Fathers (Eerdman's, Grand Rapids 1969).

Clark, S. B., *Man and Woman in Christ* (Servant Books, Ann Arbor, Michigan 1980).

Conzelmann, H., *The Theology of Saint Luke* (Faber & Faber, London 1960); *1 Corinthians* (Hermeneia Fortress, Philadelphia 1975); *Die Kleineren Briefe der Apostels Paulus* (Vandenhoeck & Ruprecht, Gottingen 1962).

Coyle, J. C., 'The Fathers on Women and Women's Ordination' *Eg.et.Th.*

9 (1978), pp.50–101.
Craig, T. C., *1 Corinthians* Interpreters Bible 1953.
Cranfield, C. E. B., *Mark* (Cambridge University Press 1959); 'St Mark 16:1–8' *SJT* 5 (1952), p.282; *Romans* Vol.II ICC (T. & T. Clark, Edinburgh 1979).
Creed, J. M., *Luke* (Macmillan, London 1957).
Cupitt, D., *Crisis of Moral Authority* (Lutterworth, London 1972).

Danielou, J., *The Ministry of Women in the Early Church* (Faith Press, London 1961).
Delling, G., *'tassō' TDNT* III, pp.27–48.
de Satgé, J. *Mary and the Christian Gospel* (SPCK, London 1976).
Dibelius, M., *The Sermon on the Mount* (Ch.Scribner's Sons, New York 1940).
Dibelius, M. & Conzelmann, H., *The Pastoral Epistles* (Hermeneia Fortress Press, Philadelphia 1972).
Dickinson, G. L., *The Greek View of Life* (Methuen, London 1957).

Easton, B. S., *The Pastoral Epistles* (SCM, London 1948).
Edersheim, A., *Sketches of Jewish Social Life in the Days of Christ* (Pickering and Inglis, London 1876).
Eichrodt, W., *Theology of the Old Testament* (SCM, London 1961).
Elliott, J. K., 'Paul's Teaching on Marriage in 1 Corinthians' *NTS* 19 (1972–73), p.219.
Ellis, E., *Luke* NCB (Oliphants, London 1974); 'Paul and His Co-Workers' *NTS* 17 (1970–71), pp.437–452.
Epstein, I., *Judaism* (Epworth Press, London 1939); edit. *The Babylonian Talmud* (Soncino, London 1948).

Feuillet, A., 'La Dignité et la Rôle de la Femme d'après Quelques Textes Pauliniens: Comparison avec l'Ancien Testament' *NTS* 21 (1975), pp.157–191; 'L'Homme "gloire de Dieu" et la Femme "gloire de l'homme"' *Rev.Bib.* 81 (1974), pp.161–182.
Filson, F. V., *Matthew* (A. & C. Black, London 1960).
Fisher, F., *1 & 2 Corinthians* (Word Books, Waco Texas 1975).
Fitzmeyer, J. A., 'A Feature of Qumran Angelology and the Angels of 1 Corinthians 11:10' *NTS* 4 (1957–58), p.48.
Foh, S. T., 'What is the Woman's Desire?' *W.Th.J.* 37 (1974), pp.376–383.
Forster, W., *Palestinian Judaism in N.T. Times* (Oliver & Boyd, Edinburgh 1964).
Foster, J., 'St Paul and Women' *Exp.T.* 62 (1951), p.376.
Foster, R. C., *Studies in the Life of Christ* (Baker, Grand Rapids 1968).
Fraser, D. S., 'Women in Ancient Israel' *JCBRF* 26 (1974), pp.29–37.
Freud, S., 'Feminity' *New Introductory Lectures on Psycho-Analysis* (Norton, N.Y. 1965).

Geldenhuys, J. N., *Luke* NLC (Marshall, Morgan & Scott, London 1950).

George, A., 'Mary' X. Leon-Dufour edit. *Dictionary of Biblical Theology* (Chapman, London 1973), pp.338–342.

Goguel, M., *The Primitive Church* (George Allen & Unwin, London 1964).

Greer, G., *A Female Eunuch* (MacGibbon & Kee, 1970).

Greig, J. C. G., 'Women's Hats – 1 Corinthians 11:1–16' *Exp.T.* 69 (1958), p.156.

Grosheide, F. W., *1 Corinthians* NLC (Marshall, Morgan & Scott, London 1954).

Guthrie, D., *Jesus the Messiah* (Zondervan, Grand Rapids 1972); *The Pastoral Epistles* (Tyndale Press, London 1957).

Haenchen, E., *Acts* (Blackwell, Oxford 1971).

Hanson, A. T., *Studies in the Pastoral Epistles* (SPCK, London 1968).

Hanson, P. D., 'Masculine Metaphors for God and Sex-Discrimination in the Old Testament' *Ecum.Rev.* 27 (1975), pp.316–324.

Harnack, A., *Luke the Physician* (Williams & Norgate, London 1907).

Harrison, P. N., *The Problem of the Pastoral Epistles* (OUP, Oxford 1956).

Harper, J., *Women and the Gospel* (CBRF, Pinner 1974).

Harvey, A. E., 'Elders' *JTS* 25 (1974), pp.318–332.

Hendriksen, W., *John* (Banner of Truth, London 1954); *Ephesians* (Banner of Truth, London 1967); *Colossians & Philemon* (Banner of Truth, London 1964); *1 & 2 Timothy & Titus* (Banner of Truth, London 1959).

Henry, C. F. H., 'Reflections on Women's Lib' *Ch.Tod.* 19 (1975), pp.345–346.

Henry, M., *Commentary* (Marshall, Morgan & Scott, London 1953).

Héring, J., *1 Corinthians* (Epworth, London 1962).

Hodge, C., *1 Corinthians* (Banner of Truth, London 1873).

Hill, D., *Matthew* (Baker, Grand Rapids 1973).

Hommes, N. J., 'Let Women Be Silent in the Churches' *Calv.Th.J.* 4 (1969), pp.5–22.

Hooker, M. D., '"Authority on her Head"; An Examination of 1 Corinthians 11:10' *NTS* 10 (1963–4), p.410.

Hunter, A. M., *Romans* (SCM, London 1955).

Hurd, J. C., *The Origin of 1 Corinthians* (SPCK, London 1965).

Hurley, J. B., 'Did Paul Require Veils or the Silence of Women?' *W.Th.J.* 35 (1972), p.190; *Man and Woman in Biblical Perspective* (IVP, London 1981); *Man and Woman in 1 Corinthians,* Unpublished doctoral thesis (Cambridge 1973).

Jacob, E., *Theology of the Old Testament* (Hodder & Stoughton, London 1958).

Jeremias, J., *Jerusalem in the Time of Jesus* (SCM, London 1969); *New Testament Theology* (SCM, London 1971).

Jervell, J., *Luke and the People of God* (Augsburg, Minneapolis 1972).

Jewett, P. K., *Man as Male and Female* (Eerdmans, Grand Rapids 1975).

Johnson, S. E., *Mark* (A. & C. Black, London 1960).
Josephus, *Antiquities* (Loeb Classical Library, Heinemann, London 1966); *Contra Apionem* (Loeb Classical Library, Heinemann, London 1966); *Jewish War* (Loeb Classical Library, Heinemann, London 1966).

Kahler, E., *Die Frau in den Paulinischen Briefen* (Gotthelf-Verlag, Zurich 1960).
Kee, H. C. & Young, F. W., *The Living World of the N.T.* (Darton, Longman & Todd, London 1960).
Kelly, J. N. D., *The Pastoral Epistles* (A. & C. Black, London 1963); *1 & 2 Peter and Jude* (A. & C. Black, London 1969).
Kidner, D., *Proverbs* (Tyndale Press, London 1964).
Kittel, G., *'exousia' TDNT* II.
Knight, G. W., 'Male and Female Related He Them' *Ch.Tod.* 21 (1976), pp.709–713; *The N.T. Teaching on the Role Relationship of Male and Female* (Baker, Grand Rapids 1977).
Koehler, L., *Old Testament Theology* (Lutterworth, London 1957).
Kümmel, W. G., *The Theology of the New Testament* (SCM, London 1974); *Man in the New Testament* (Epworth, London 1963).
Küng, H., *On Being a Christian* (Collins, London 1977).

Ladd, G. E., *A Theology of the New Testament* (Eerdmans, Grand Rapids 1974).
Lane, W. L., *Mark* NLC (Marshall, Morgan & Scott, London 1974).
Leaney, A. R. C., *Luke* (A. & C. Black, London 1958); *Timothy, Titus & Philemon* (SCM, London 1960).
Leenhardt, F. J., *Romans* (Lutterworth, London 1961).
Leupold, H. C., *Exposition of Genesis* (Wartburg, Ohio 1942).
Lewis, C. S., 'Priestesses in the Church?' W. Hooper edit. *God in the Dock* (Eerdmans, Grand Rapids 1970).
Lietzmann, H., *An die Korinther* (Mohr, Tubingen 1969).
Lindars, B., *John* (Oliphants, London 1972).
Lohse, E., *Colossians and Philemon* (Hermeneia, Fortress Press, Philadelphia 1971); *Umwelt des Neuen Testaments* (Vandenhoeck & Ruprecht, Gottingen 1974).
Luther, M., *Works* Vol. I (Concordia, St. Louis 1958).

Mace, D. R., *Hebrew Marriage* (Epworth, London 1953).
Marsh, J., *John* (Penguin, Harmondsworth 1968).
Marshall, I. H., *Luke, Historian and Theologian* (Paternoster, Exeter 1970).
Martin, R. P., *1 Corinthians – Galatians* (Scripture Union, London 1968); *Colossians and Philemon* NCB (Oliphants, London 1974).
Martin, W. J., '1 Corinthians 11:2–16; An Interpretation' W. W. Gasque & R. P. Martin edit. *Apostolic History and the Gospel* (Paternoster, Exeter 1970).
McArthur, H. K., edit. *In Search of the Historical Jesus* (SPCK, London 1970).

McGlashan, R., 'Diakonia and the Diaconate' *Ch.* 84 (1970), pp.7–14, 126–129 .

McHugh, J., *The Mother of Jesus in the New Testament* (Darton, Longman & Todd, London 1975).

McKeating, H., 'Jesus ben Sira's Attitude to Women' *Exp.T.* 85 (1973), p.85.

McKenzie, J. L., *A Theology of the Old Testament* (Chapman, New York 1974).

Meeks, W. A., 'The Image of the Androgyne; Some Uses of a Symbol in Earliest Christianity' *Hist.Rel.* 13 (1974), pp.165–208.

Mendelsohn, I., 'The Family in the Ancient Near East' *Bib.Arch.* 11 (1948).

Miller, J. M., 'In the Image and Likeness of God' *JBL* 91 (1972), p.289.

Millett, K., *Sexual Politics* (Doubleday, New York 1970).

Mitton, C. L., *Ephesians* NCB (Oliphants, London 1976).

Montefiore, C. G. & Loewe, H., *A Rabbinic Anthology* (Meridian, USA 1938).

Montefiore, C. G., *The Synoptic Gospels* (Macmillan, London 1909).

Moo, D. J., '1 Timothy 2:11–15; Meaning and Significance' *Trinity Journal* 1 (1980), pp.62–83; 'The Interpretation of 1 Timothy 2:11–15: A Rejoinder' *Trinity Journal* 2 (1981), pp.198–222.

Moore, G. F., *Judaism* (Harvard Univ. Press, Cambridge, Mass. 1958).

Morris, L., *Luke* (IVP, London 1974); *John* NLC (Marshall, Morgan & Scott, London 1971); *1 Corinthians* (Tyndale Press, London 1958).

Moule, C. F. D., *The Phenomenon of the New Testament* (SCM, London 1967); *Worship in the New Testament* (Lutterworth, London 1961); *Colossians and Philemon* (CUP, Cambridge 1957).

Muilenburg, J., 'Form Citicism and Beyond' *JBL* 88 (1969), pp.1–18.

Murray, J., *Romans* NLC (Marshall, Morgan & Scott, London 1967).

Neil, W., *Acts* NCB (Oliphants, London 1973).

Noth, M., *Numbers* (SCM, London 1968).

Nygren, A., *Romans* (SCM, London 1952).

Oepke, A., '*gunē*' *TDNT* I.

Oesterley, H. O. E. & Box, G. H., *The Religion and Worship of the Synagogue* (Pitman, London 1911).

Osborne, G. R., 'Hermeneutics and Women in the Church' *JETS* 20 (1977), pp.337–352.

Payne, J. B., *The Theology of the Older Testament* (Zondervan, Grand Rapids 1962); 'Libertarian Women in Ephesus: A Response to D. J. Moo's Article "1 Timothy 2:11–15; Meaning and Significance"' *Trinity Journal* 2 (1981), pp.169–197.

Pagels, E. H., 'Paul and Women: A Response to Recent Discussion' *JAAR* 42 (1974), pp.538–549.

Pedersen, J., *Israel, Its Life and Culture* (OUP, London 1926);

Philo, *Hypothetica* (The Loeb Classical Library, W. Heinemann,

London 1971); *De Specialibus Legibus* (The Loeb Classical Library, W. Heinemann, London 1971).

Pliny, *Natural History* (The Loeb Classical Library, W. Heinemann, London 1971); *Letters* (The Loeb Classical Library, W. Heinemann, London 1971).

Piper, O. A., *The Christian Interpretation of Sex* (Ch.Scribner's Sons, New York 1941).

Powers, B. W., 'Women in the Church: The Application of 1 Timothy 2:8–15' *Interchange* 17 (1975), pp.55–59.

Pritchard, J. B., edit. *Ancient Near Eastern Texts Relating to the Old Testament* (Princeton University Press 1969).

Rahner, K., *Theological Investigations* I (Darton, Longman & Todd, London 1974).

Rengstorf, K. H., *'apostolos' TDNT* I; 'oikodespoteō/ēs' *TDNT* II.

Reynolds, S. A., 'On Head Coverings' *W.Th.J.* 36 (1973), pp.90–91.

Robertson, A. & Plummer, A., *1 Corinthians* ICC (T. & T. Clark, Edinburgh 1914).

Robinson, H. W., *The Christian Doctrine of Man* (T. & T. Clark, Edinburgh 1926).

Robinson, J. M., *A New Quest for the Historical Jesus* (SCM, London 1959).

Roth, C., 'Were the Qumran Sectaries Essene?' *JTS* 10 (1959), p.87.

Sampley, J. P., *And the Two Shall Become One Flesh* SNTS Monograph 16 (CUP 1971).

Scanzoni, L. & Hardesty, N., *All We're Meant To Be* (Word Books, Waco Texas 1974).

Schlier, H., *'kephalē' TDNT* III.

Schmithals, W., *The Office of Apostle in the Early Church* (SPCK, London 1971).

Schürer, E., *A History of the Jewish People in the Time of Jesus Christ* (Ch.Scribner's Sons, New York 1890).

Schütz, J. H., *Paul and the Anatomy of Apostolic Authority* (CUP, Cambridge 1975).

Schweizer, E., *Church Order in the New Testament* (SCM, London 1971); *Matthew* (SPCK, London 1975); *Mark* (SPCK, London 1971).

Scott, A., *Christianity According to Saint Paul* (CUP, Cambridge 1932).

Scroggs, P., 'Paul and the Eschatological Woman' *JAAR* 40 (1972).

Scullard, H. H., *From the Gracchi to Nero* (Methuen, London 1959).

Selwyn, E. G., *1 Peter* (Macmillan, London 1946).

Shea, M. C., 'Cana' *The Downside Review* 95 (1977).

Simpson, E. K. & Bruce, F. F., *Ephesians and Colossians* NLC (Marshall, Morgan and Scott, London 1957).

Skinner, J., *Genesis* ICC (T. & T. Clark, Edinburgh 1930).

Smith, C. R., *The Bible Doctrine of Man* (Epworth, London 1951); *The Bible Doctrine of Womanhood* (Epworth, London 1923).

Sparks, H. F. D., 'The Books of the Qumran Community' *JTS* 6 (1955), p.226.

Spencer, A. D. B., 'Eve at Ephesus' *JETS* 17 (1974), pp.215–222.

Spicq, C., *Saint Pierre* (Gabalda, Paris 1966).

Stacey, W. D., *The Pauline View of Man* (Macmillan, New York 1956).

Stanton, G. N., *Jesus of Nazareth in New Testament Preaching* (CUP, Cambridge 1974).

Stendahl, K., *The Bible and the Role of Women* (Fortress Press, Philadelphia 1966).

Stibbs, A., *1 Peter* (IVP, London 1959); '1 Timothy' D. Guthrie & J. A. Motyer edit. *New Bible Commentary (Revised)* (IVP, London 1970).

Tarn, W. W., *Hellenistic Civilization* (Arnold, London 1930).

Tavard, G. H., *Women in Christian Tradition* (University Press, Notre Dame, Ind. 1973).

Taylor, G., 'Woman in Creation and Redemption' *JCBRF* 26 (1974), pp.14–28.

Taylor, V., *Mark* (Macmillan, London 1966).

Temple, W., *Readings in St John's Gospel* (Macmillan, London 1945).

Tenney, M. C., *Galatians* (Pickering & Inglis, London 1950).

Thielicke, H., *How the World Began* (Muhlenberg, Philadelphia 1961).

Thomas, W., 'The Place of Women in the Church at Philippi' *Exp.T.* 83 (1972), pp.117–120.

Thrall, M., *The Ordination of Women to the Priesthood* (SCM, London 1958).

Timiadis, E., 'From the Margin to the Forefront' *Ecum.Rev.* 27 (1975), pp.366–373.

Trible, P., 'Depatriarchalizing in Biblical Interpretation' *JAAR* 41 (1973).

Vogels, W., 'It is not good that the "Mensch" should be alone; I will make him/her a helper fit for him/her' *Ég.et.Th.* 9 (1978), pp.9–35.

von Rad, G., *Genesis* (SCM, London 1972).

Vos, C. J., *Woman in Old Testament Worship* (Judels & Brinkman, Delft 1968).

Vriezen, T. C., *An Outline of Old Testament Theology* (Blackwell, Oxford 1970).

Walker, W. O., '1 Corinthians 11:2–16 and Paul's Views Regarding Women' *JBL* 94 (1975), p.94.

Ward, R. A., *1 & 2 Timothy and Titus* (Word Books, Waco Texas 1974).

Weeks, N., 'Of Silence and Head Covering' *W.Th.J.* 35 (1972), pp.22–27.

Westermann, C., *Creation* (SPCK, London 1974).

Williams, C. S. C., *Acts* (A. & C. Black, London 1957).

Wolff, H. W., *Anthropology of the Old Testament* (SCM, London 1974).

Woolf, B. L., *The Background and Beginnings of the Gospel Story* (Nicholson & Watson, London 1935).

Zabolai-Caekme, E., 'A Woman Looks at Theology' *Ecum.Rev.* 27 (1975), pp.316–324.

Notes

INTRODUCTION
(pages 9 – 10)

1 S. Freud, 'Femininity' *New Introductory Lectures on Psycho-Analysis*, p.113.
2 For example, the influence of the Aristotelian dualistic world view has been very strong, and only questioned comparatively recently. This view sees the world in terms of opposing forces and ideas, e.g. active, strong, stable, male, above, good – as opposed to passive, weak, fickle, female, below, evil.

CHAPTER ONE

(pages 11 – 32)

1 G. von Rad, *Genesis*, p.60.
2 H. Thielicke, *How the World Began*, p.89. Some would in fact see here a reference to the androgynous myth that the first human being was a bi-sexual creature later split into two, but the pronouns used here, 'him' followed by 'them' make this unlikely and in any case the terms used here are specifically those used for male and female people rather than for qualities of masculinity and femininity. However cf note 16, p.143 below.
3 H. W. Wolff, *Anthropology of the Old Testament*, p.94.
4 P. K. Jewett, *Man as Male and Female*, pp.24–40.
5 'For how can it be said of woman that she is the image of God?' Ambrosiaster *Liber quaestionum veteris et noui testamenti* 45:3 (C.S.E.L. 50, p.83–4). Or 'It is evident that a female...is not an image of God, not even as regards her soul' Diodore of Tarsus *Fragmentum in Gen. 1:26* (P.G. 33 col 1564C) as quoted in J. C. Coyle, 'The Fathers on Women and Women's Ordination', Église et Théologie 9 (1978), pp.51–101.
6 T. Aquinas, *Summa Theologica* Q93.
7 K. Barth, *Church Dogmatics* III, p.196.
8 C. J. Vos, *Women in Old Testament Worship*, p.15.
9 Augustine (*De Trinitatas* 7:10) holds to a three-fold pattern of self-love,

self-knowledge and memory. Whatever characteristics are seen as resulting from Man being in the image of God, it is probably wise to heed von Rad's warning against making an anachronistic dichotomy between physical and spiritual likeness, which would be false to ancient oriental thinking. (See *TDNT*, εἰχων, D. The Divine Likeness in the Old Testament, pp.390–392.)

10 J. Calvin, *Genesis*, p.129.
11 P. Trible, 'Depatriarchalizing in Biblical Interpretation', *JAAR* 41 (1973), pp.36–37, cf J. Muilenburg, 'Form Criticism and Beyond', *JBL* 88 (1969), p.9f.
12 J. Calvin, *Pastoral Epistles*, p.70.
13 cf pp.100–107 below.
14 E. Jacob, *Theology of the Old Testament*, p.73. Margaret Thrall in *The Ordination of Woman to the Priesthood* also accepts from this that Genesis 2 implies that woman has only a derivative existence in the image of God.
15 Making the 'as in Adam' argument of 1 Corinthians 15:22 meaningful for women as well as men.
16 W. Vogels ('It is not Good that the "Mensch" should be alone; I Will Make Him/Her a Helper Fit for Him/Her', *Église et Théologie* 9 (1978), pp.9–35) argues that as the word for a male (*ish*) is not used until verse 23 after the creation of the woman, it is not appropriate to consider the original being as a male rather than simply as a person. The word *adam*, which is used exclusively up to verse 23, and which later becomes also the proper name for the man Adam, is the general term for mankind applicable to both men and women and equivalent to the German word *mensch*. Hence the translation of verse 18 which forms the title of Vogels' article.
17 G. Taylor, 'Woman in Creation and Redemption' *JCBRF* 26 (1974), p.18.
18 P. Trible, *art.cit*, p.37.
19 cf also Gen. 3:20, 4:17, etc.,
20 G. W. Knight, 'Male and Female Related He Them', *Ch.Tod*. 21, 1976, p.710.
21 T. C. Vriezen, *An Outline of Old Testament Theology*, p.411.
22 Isaiah 30:5, Ezekiel 12:14, Deuteronomy 11:34.
23 e.g. Exodus 18:4, Psalm 121:2. cf C. J. Vos *op.cit.*, p.16.
24 'I do not see in what way it could be said that woman was made a help for man if the work of childbearing be excluded.' *De Genesi ad Litteram* IX.5, cf VII.3.
25 P. K. Jewett, *op.cit.*, p.126.
26 J. Pedersen, *Israel, Its Life and Culture*, p.68.
27 That is, the theory that apart from the obvious necessities of procreation, sex differences have no essential role to play in society and that therefore a society composed entirely of one sex could exist in a perfectly satisfactory fashion. cf G. Greer, *The Female Eunuch:* Woman 'should be self-sufficient and consciously refrain from establishing exclusive dependencies,' p.18; and J. Johnson, *The Lesbian Nation*, who advocates separatism. It is interesting to note the basic similarity between this view, and Augustine's picture of a society where women's 'help' consists only of child-bearing.
28 C. Westermann, *Creation*, p.86.
29 e.g. M. Luther: 'The subtlety of Satan showed itself also when he attacked human nature where it was weakest... I believe that had Satan first tempted the man, Adam would have gained the victory', *Genesis*, p.68.
30 H. C. Leupold, *Exposition of Genesis*, p.173.
31 C. Westermann, *op.cit.*, p.93.
32 J. Skinner, *Genesis*, p.82.
33 C. Vos, *op.cit.*, p.24.

34 J. Calvin, *op.cit.*, p.172.
35 Genesis 3:16; 4:7. Ct. 7:10.
36 S. Foh, 'What is the Woman's Desire?' *W.Th.J.* 37 (1974), pp.376–385.
37 S. Foh, *op.cit.*, p.382.
38 M. Luther, *op.cit.*, p.200.
39 D. S. Bailey, *The Man-Woman Relation in Christian Thought*, p.288.
40 J. A. Bailey, 'Initiation and the Primal Woman in Gilgamesh and Genesis 2–3', *JBL* 89 (1970), pp.149–150.
41 E. Zabolai-Caekme, 'A Woman looks at Theology', *Ecum.Rev.* 27 (1975), p.325.
42 C. J. Vos, *Women in Old Testament Worship*, p.38.
43 P. Trible, 'Depatriarchalizing in Biblical Interpretation', *JAAR* 41 (1973), p.31.
44 C. J. Vos, *op.cit.*, p.39. It must be noted here that the use of the masculine in pronouns as opposed to other imagery is not strictly relevant. One or the other has to be used, and as in English the masculine is primary and can be used generically. It would be wrong to assume from this, that the use of the masculine is incidental, that the feminine pronoun could equally well have been used and that God can appropriately be described as 'She'. The use of the feminine pronoun would specify gender in a way that the use of the masculine does not.
45 P. D. Hanson, 'Masculine Metaphors for God and Sex-discrimination in the Old Testament', *Ecum.Rev.* 27 (1975), p.317.
46 G. Taylor, 'Woman in Creation and Redemption', *JCBRF* 26 (1974), p.15. C. S. Lewis, *God in the Dock*, p.237, bases his argument for the essential masculinity (although not sexuality) of God on the use of masculine terminology. This does not take into account the occasions where feminine terminology is in fact discovered.
47 Exodus 16:4–36; Psalm 36:8; Hosea 11:4, etc.
48 Nehemiah 9:15; Exodus 17:1–7, etc.
49 Nehemiah 9:21.
50 M. Noth, *Numbers*, p.86.
51 e.g. Isaiah 42:14; 49:15; 66:9, 13; Psalm 22:9–10; 71:6.
52 Exodus 22:21–27, etc.
53 Isaiah 61:1.
54 P. Hanson, *op.cit.*, p.318.
55 D. S. Fraser, 'Woman in Ancient Israel', *JCBRF* 26 (1974), p.32.
56 cf, p.24 below.
57 Though this must not be taken as implying that they were not also very well aware of the concept of individuality both of men and women. cf J. W. Rogerson, 'The Hebrew concept of Corporate Personality: A Re-Examination' *JTS* 21 (1970), pp.1–16.
58 cf Jeremiah 8:21.
59 P. Trible, *op.cit.*, pp.42–47.
60 C. Ryder Smith, *The Bible Doctrine of Womanhood*, pp.48–49.
61 The existence of lone widows like Ruth and Naomi indicates that there were exceptions to this rule and this perhaps shows the danger of trying to build up too structured a picture of Old Testament life. There are always those who do not quite fit into the overall pattern.
62 D. R. Mace, *Hebrew Marriage*, pp.184–186.
63 Sarah's fear of Hagar in Genesis 16:4–6 makes sense in this situation.
64 D. R. Mace, *op.cit.*, p.191.
65 C. J. Vos, *Woman in Old Testament Worship*, p.46.
66 J. Pedersen, *Israel – Its Life and Culture*, p.76.

67 cf Genesis 12:11–13; 19:8; Judges 19:24.
68 J. Pedersen, *op.cit.*, p.63, p.76.
69 Psalm 128; Ezekiel 19:10 etc.
70 Proverbs 12:4; 14:1; 19:14; 31:10–34.
71 D. Kidner, *Proverbs*, p.183.
72 I. Mendelsohn, 'The Family in the Ancient Near East', *Bib.Arch.* 11 (1948).
73 J. B. Pritchard, edit., *Ancient Near Eastern Texts Relating to the Old Testament*, pp.172–4.
74 J. L. McKenzie, *A Theology of the Old Testament*, p.228.
75 T. C. Vriezen, *An Outline of Old Testament Theology*, p.120. cf A. Reifenberg, *Ancient Hebrew Seals* (1950).
76 D. R. Mace, *op.cit.* p.189.
77 W. Eichrodt, *Theology of the Old Testament*, p.81.
78 L. Koehler, *Old Testament Theology*, p.69.
79 W. Eichrodt, *op.cit.*, p.131.
80 P.K. Jewett, *Man as Male and Female*, p.86.
81 Deuteronomy 5:29,33. etc.
82 C. J. Vos, *op.cit.*, p.131.
83 C. J. Vos, *op.cit.*, pp.51–59.
84 J. Calvin, *Corpus Reformatorum* LI p.453.
85 1 Samuel 17:26; Judges 14:3; Exodus 12:48.
86 Deuteronomy 31:12–13; cf Joshua 8:35; Nehemiah 8:2f.
87 2 Chronicles 15:12–13; Deuteronomy 17:2–5; 29:18–21.
88 Deuteronomy 13:6–11.
89 Dealing with cleansing after the birth of a child or after any other female uncleanness.
90 C. J. Vos, *op.cit.* p.130.
91 Exodus 35:22.
92 Exodus 23:17; 34:23; Deuteronomy 16:16.
93 cf J. B. Payne, *The Theology of the Older Testament* p.229, W. Eichrodt, *op.cit.* p.131, Oesterley and Box, *The Religion and Worship of the Synagogue* pp.326–7.
94 cf Deuteronomy 12:12,18; 16:11,14.
95 e.g. Rebekah in Genesis 25:22, Rachel in Genesis 30:6,22, and Hannah in 1 Samuel 1:10.
96 C. J. Vos, *op.cit.*, p.201. cf Numbers 6:2–20.
97 Exodus 38:8, 1 Samuel 2:22. The suggestion that they were cult prostitutes is unlikely, as if so, their being mentioned without the very strong condemnation found elsewhere in the Old Testament would be most unusual.
98 C. J. Vos, *op.cit.*, p.159.
99 Exodus 15:20; 1 Samuel 18:6; 2 Samuel 6:14; Psalm 30:11; Jeremiah 31:4, etc.
100 Exodus 15:21; Judges 5:1; 1 Chronicles 25:5; 2 Chronicles 35:5; Ezra 2:65.
101 J. B. Payne, *op.cit.*, p.229.
102 J. B. Payne, *The Theology of the Older Testament*, p.229.
103 E. Jacob, *Theology of the Old Testament*, p.173.
104 e.g. Leviticus 22:13.
105 J. Calvin, *Corpus Reformatorum*, Vol. LXVIII.
106 C. J. Vos, *Women in Old Testament Worship*, p.208.
107 2 Kings 22:14f.
108 C. J. Vos, *op.cit.*, p.186.
109 Nehemiah 6:14; Ezekiel 13:17f.
110 E. Jacob, *op.cit.*, p.251.
111 Judges 5:28–30; 2 Samuel 14:2ff; 20:16ff. etc.

112 C. J. Vos, *op.cit.*, p.209.
113 K. Millett, *Sexual Politics*, p.51.
114 P. Trible, 'Depatriarchalizing in Biblical Interpretation', JAAR 41 (1973), p.31.

CHAPTER TWO

(pages 33 – 43)

1   C. G. Montefiiore and H. Loewe, *A Rabbinic Anthology*, p.510.
2   cf Ket. 30a; Meg. 14b; Nidd. 45b.
3   cf Sanh. 7a; Shab. 33b; Kidd 49b; Ket. 59b,65a.
4   Shab. 33b.
5   J. Jeremias, *Jerusalem in the Time of Jesus*, p.375.
6   Contra Apionem 24:201.
7   I. Epstein, *Judaism*, p.53.
8   cf Yeb. 63a,63b.
9   Yeb. 44a,65a; Ket. 52b.
10 Yeb. 63b; Gitt. 9:10.
11 J. Jeremias, *op.cit.*, pp.369–370.
12 D. S. Bailey, *The Man-Woman Relation in Christian Thought*, p.2.
13 W. E. Oesterley and G. H. Box, *The Religion and Worship of the Synagogue*, p.326.
14 B.M. 59a; Jeb. 62b.
15 W. Forster, *Palestinian Judaism in New Testament Times*, p.128.
16 *Hypothetica*, 7:3. The Greek word used here, *Douleusin*, could be translated as 'slavery'.
17 W. Forster, *op.cit.*, p.219
18 Ecclesiasticus 36:24; 40:23.
19 *De Specialibus Legibus*, 3.169.
20 Yeb. 77a.
21 e.g. Acts 18:3.
22 Queen Alexandra kept power in her hands for nine years 76–67 BC and Salome danced before her step-father's guests.
23 A. Edersheim, *Sketches of Jewish Social Life in the Days of Christ*, p.139.
24 cf J. Jeremias, *op.cit.*, pp.361–363.
25 W. Forster, *op.cit.*, p.129.
26 M. McKeating, 'Jesus ben Sirach's Attitude to Women', *Exp.T.* 85 (1973), p.85.
27 Ned. 20a.
28 John 4:27.
29 Ber. 61a.
30 J. Jeremias, *op.cit.*, p.372.
31 Ket. 59b.
32 Shebu 4:1; Yeb. 16:7; B.K. 88a.
33 R.Sh. 1:8.
34 cf J. Jeremias, *op.cit.*, p.372.
35 *Antiquities*, 4:219.
36 W. E. Oesterley and G. H. Box, *op.cit.*, p.327.
37 Ber. 45b.
38 Hag. 3a.
39 G. F. Moore, *Judaism II*, p.131, cf Meg. 23a.
40 *idem*, p.46.

41 There is no gallery in the Mesopotamian synagogue of Dura-Europos which was built as late as 245 AD.
42 E. Schurer, *A History of the Jewish People at the Time of Jesus Christ*, p.75.
43 W. A. Meeks, 'The Image of the Androgyne', *Hist.Rel.* 13, p.165.
44 Sot. 19a.
45 Yom. 66b.
46 Pes. 62b.
47 G. F. Moore *op.cit.*, cf Tos Kelimii 1:6; Ber. 10a.
48 E. Lohse, *Umwelt Des Neuen Testaments*, p.107.
49 H. F. D. Sparks, 'The Books of the Qumran Community', *JTS* 6 (1955), p.226.
50 C. Roth, 'Were the Qumran Sectaries Essene?' *JTS* 10 (1959), p.87.
51 *Hypothetica* 11:14–17.
52 *Jewish War* 2:120.
53 *Natural History* 5:15.
54 *Jewish War* 2:160f.
55 E. Lohse, *Umwelt Des Neuen Testaments*, p.60.
56 W. A. Meeks, 'The Image of the Androgyne', *Hist.Rel.* 13 (1974), p.165. cf 1 QS 1:9, 1:10; 2:2; 5:1f.
57 cf 1 QSa 1:4ff.
58 1 QSa 1:8–11.
59 W. A. Meeks, *art.cit.*, cf 1 QSa 1:11.
60 CD 7:6–9; 14:13ff.
61 F. F. Bruce, *New Testament History*, p.102, cf *Second Thoughts on the Dead Sea Scrolls*, pp.46,106.
62 CD 4.
63 CD 16.
64 H. H. Scullard, *From the Gracchi to Nero*, p.181.
65 B. L. Woolf, *The Background and Beginning of the Gospel Story*, p.99.
66 *idem* , p.99.
67 G. L. Dickinson, *The Greek View of Life*, p.170.
68 *idem* , p.176.
69 B. L. Woolf, *op.cit.*, p.99.
70 D. S. Bailey, *The Man–Woman Relation in Christian Thought*, p.4.
71 W. A. Meeks, 'The Image of the Androgyne,' *Hist.Rel.* 13 (1974), pp.165–208.
72 D. S. Bailey, *op.cit.*, p.3.
73 W. A. Meeks, *op.cit.*, p.170.
74 B. L. Woolf, *op.cit.*, p.101.
75 W. W. Tarn, *Hellenistic Civilization*, p.91.
76 W. A. Meeks, *art.cit.*, of Epictetus *Discourses* 1.16; 9–14 III1; 24–25 and pseudo-Phocyclides 212.
77 D. S. Bailey, *op.cit.*, p.4.
78 *idem.*
79 H. H. Scullard, *op.cit.*, p.182.
80 *idem* , p.238.
81 D. S. Bailey, *op.cit.*, p.4.
82 *idem* , p.5.
83 cf H. Scullard, *op.cit.*, p.183.
84 D. S. Bailey, *op.cit.*, p.3.
85 D. S. Bailey, *The Man-Woman Relation in Christian Thought*, pp.5–6.
86 *idem*, p.7.
87 W. D. Davies, *Christian Origins and Judaism*, p.220.

CHAPTER THREE

(pages 44 – 60)

1 W. Forster, *Palestinian Judaism in New Testament Times*, p.127.

2 J. Jeremias, New Testament Theology Vol.1, p.27.

3 e.g. I. H. Marshall, *Luke, Historian and Theologian*, p.139; D. Guthrie, *Jesus the Messiah*, p.155f; A. Harnack, *Luke the Physician*, p.155 who points out that 'A very considerable portion of the matter peculiar to St Luke is... feminine in interest.' Though H. Conzelmann, *The Theology of St Luke*, p.46f, does suggest that Luke is interested in women primarily because of their importance as witnesses distinct from the apostles, present at all the different stages of Luke's account.

4 e.g. Luke 7:36–50; 13:10–17.

5 R. E. Brown, 'Roles of Women in the Fourth Gospel', *Th.St.* 36 (1975), p.699. 'In researching the evidence of the fourth Gospel, one is still surprised to see to what extent in the Johannine community women and men were already on an equal level in the fold of the Good Shepherd. This seems to have been a community where in the things that really mattered in the following of Christ there was no difference between male and female.'

6 e.g. John 11:21–23.

7 e.g. Luke 11:27–28.

8 cf C. D. Moule, *The Phenomenon of the New Testament*, p.65.

9 cf pp.33–43, above.

10 G. N. Stanton, *Jesus of Nazareth in New Testament Preaching*, p.152. It has been questioned whether it is possible to create any portrait of the historical Jesus. Bultmann argued that it was not, because 'his form-critical research tended to confirm the view that such a quest is impossible and his existential theology carried through the thesis that such a quest is illegitimate.' J. M. Robinson, *A New Quest for the Historical Jesus*, p.12. The extent of the discussion concerning this can be seen in H. K. McArthur (edit.), *In Search of the Historical Jesus*. However, the fact that Jesus' attitude on this point was so 'startlingly new', and the consistency of the portrait – with evidence obtained from all the different forms and sources identified by the critics, and from all four gospels – is a strong indication that here at least there is authenticity.

11 Although some would see Matthew 5–7 not as a sermon given by Jesus on a single occasion but rather as 'a summary of characteristic sayings whose origin we do not know ' (M. Dibelius, *The Sermon on the Mount*, p.42), nevertheless there is general agreement that it does accurately represent the teaching of Jesus.

12 J. Jeremias, *op.cit.*, p.226, cf p.34 above.

13 E. Schweizer, *The Good News According to Matthew*, pp.120–122. cf W. F. Albright and C. S. Mann, *Matthew*, Anchor Bible, ad loc.

14 J. Jeremias, *op.cit.*, p.227.

15 Matthew 19:4–9; 5:31,32; Mark 10:10–12; Luke 16:18.

16 Matthew 19:29; Mark 10:29. J. Bowman (*Mark*) questions whether Mark 10:29 was in fact spoken by Jesus, but the unfamiliarity of this concept makes it likely that the words of Jesus himself are being quoted as W. Lane on *Mark* and F. V. Filson on *Matthew* ad loc. would suggest.

17 This addition has no other textual support and therefore appears to be a deliberate addition by Marcion, though two Latin versions do have a similar addition to verse 5. However, though clearly not part of the text it may refer to a tradition which was known to Marcion.

18 G. L. Stanton, *Jesus of Nazareth in New Testament Preaching*, p.151.
19 Matthew 9:18–26; Mark 5:25–34; cf J. Bowman, *Mark*, ad loc.
20 Leviticus 15:25–30.
21 Luke 11:38.
22 Luke 13:10–17; Mark 1:29–31.
23 C. F. D. Moule, *The Phenomenon of the New Testament*, p.65.
24 D. S. Bailey, *The Man-Woman Relation in Christian Thought*. Bailey prefers the use of the word venereal for any aspects of sex relating to sexual desire, so that the word sexual can then be used in its more general sense.
25 cf E. Schweizer, *The Good News According to Mark* on Mark 1:31; V. Taylor, *Mark*, p.179.
26 cf A. Feuillet, 'La Dignité et la Rôle de la Femme', *NTS* 21 (1975), pp.157–191.
27 John 8:2–11. The textual evidence makes it very unlikely that this section was originally part of John's gospel, but it is undoubtedly very ancient, and as Lindars points out, 'There is no reason to doubt that an authentic tradition lies behind this story' (*John*, pp.305–306). cf L. Morris, *John*, pp.882–883. William Temple thought that the style is Lukan and that those manuscripts which place this section at the end of Luke 21 are in fact correct (*Readings in St John's Gospel*, p.150).
28 Luke 7:37. This occasion appears to be distinct from the anointing of Jesus as recorded in Matthew 26:7–13; Mark 14:3–9 and John 12:1–11. There is no reason why similar events should not have occurred, and apart from the actual fact of the anointing almost every aspect is dissimilar, e.g. an unknown sinner probably in Galilee as opposed to Mary in Bethany. J. N. Geldenhuys, *Luke*, pp.234–235, and L. Morris, *Luke*, p.146, take this view, although A. R. C. Leaney, *Luke*, p.146, sees Luke and John as parallel with Mark distinct. J. M. Creed and M. Conzelmann both assume that all four accounts are variations of the same incident.
29 John 4.
30 G. B. Caird, *Luke*, ad loc.
31 These verses have also been seen as a refusal on the part of Jesus to affirm motherhood as the primary role of women but this, although it is possible, does not seem to be the main intention of the passage. cf L. Scanzoni and N. Hardesty, *All We're Meant To Be*, p.177.
32 cf G. H. Tavard, *Women in Christian Tradition*, p.137.
33 G. N. Stanton, *Jesus of Nazareth in New Testament Preaching*, p.151.
34 Matthew 27:55; Mark 15:41; Luke 8:1–3. cf A. R. C. Leaney, *Luke*, p.149, J. M. Creed, *Luke*, p.112.
35 *Adv.Cels.* 3:10.
36 For discussion of the nature of apostleship cf W. Schmithals, *The Office of Apostle in the Early Church*; C. Brown, 'Apostle', *DNTT*, pp.126–137; K. W. Rengstorf, 'apostolos' *TDNT* 1, pp.407–445; and J. H. Schutz, *Paul and the Anatomy of Apostolic Authority*.
37 cf Matthew 19:28, 'You who have followed me will also sit on twelve thrones judging the twelve tribes of Israel.' J. Jervell, *Luke and the People of God* pp.75–112, takes the view that Luke is here describing the eschatological ruling of the nation Israel, which would explain the apostolate being Jewish and masculine. It is possible that in this instance Jervell is correct although the majority of scholars would not support his view that Luke does not at any time present the Church as the new Israel.
38 G. C. Blum, 'The Office of Woman in the New Testament', *Ch.* 85 (1971), pp.175–189.
39 Luke 10:1. This can be only conjecture as we are given no detailed information

about the seventy.

40 R. Brown, 'Roles of Women in the Fourth Gospel' *Th.St.* 36 (1975), p.692.
41 W. F. Arndt, *Luke*, commenting on Luke 8:1–3.
42 H. Beyer, TDNT Vol. II, p.81.
43 *idem*.
44 Raymond Brown is of the opinion that the use of *diakonein* in relation to the women is particularly significant in the light of the fact that the gospels were written in the latter half of the first cenutry, in John's case as late as the 90's 'when the office of *diakonos* already existed in the post-Pauline churches...and when the task of waiting on tables was a specific function to which the community or its leaders appointed individuals by laying on of hands. (Acts 6:1–6.)', *art.cit.*, p.690.
45 cf Origen, *op.cit.*
46 D. Hill, *Matthew*, pp.253–4, suggests that 'this pericope was employed for the guidance of the Matthean Church in its relation to Gentiles' and S. E. Johnson, *Mark*, pp.135–8, also stresses that Mark uses the account specifically to give help in relation to the treatment of Gentiles. However it is quite possible that it was used also for the guidance of the churches in relation to their attitude to women.
47 R. Bultmann, *John*, p.193. Bultmann is more concerned with the purpose of the account than with its historicity. He sees it as an indication of the fact that an 'encounter with him (Jesus) means a radical reversal of normal standards', p.180.
48 vv.11–15.
49 R. Brown, 'Roles of Women in the Fourth Gospel', *Th.St.* 36 (1975), p.691. Brown deals with the objection that the Samaritans' faith ultimately rested on Jesus' word and not that of the woman by pointing out that 'this is scarcely because of any inferiority she might have as a women – it is the inferiority of any human witness compared to encountering Jesus himself.'
50 E. Ellis, *Luke*, ad loc. cf J. M. Creed, *Luke*, p.154.
51 Neither Martha's original words nor her reference to Jesus as 'The Teacher' of themselves indicates necessarily any previous specific teaching, but her manner, and the ease with which new teaching is introduced here make it clear that such teaching sessions had taken place. Bultmann, *op.cit.*, p.402, thinks that this account gives us 'simply a picture of faith...not the delineation of an individual' and B. Lindars, *John*, p.386, thinks that John has fused several stories into this account and therefore he questions its historicity as it stands. However, the characters of Martha and Mary seen here are consistent with what we find in Luke 10 and there seems little reason to doubt their existence as individuals. cf L. Morris, *John*, p.537.
52 cf R. Brown, *art.cit.*, p.693.
53 John's account refers to anointing the feet rather than the head, but nevertheless these all seem to refer to the same incident, as opposed to Luke 7:37–50. cf note 28, p.149 above.
54 e.g. Filson on Matthew, Lane and Cranfield on Mark and Bultmann on John.
55 e.g. Argyle on Matthew, Schweizer on Mark, and Morris and Hendriksen on John.
56 J. Marsh, *John*, on John 11:28.
57 Luke 24:34. Paul in 1 Corinthians 15:5 follows Luke, but it is possible that in both instances the women were not mentioned simply because only the testimony of men carried weight.
58 C. E. B. Cranfield, *Mark*, p.463.
59 cf discussion on page 35 above.
60 W. L. Lane on Mark 15:40–41.

61 C. E. B. Cranfield, *op.cit.*, p.464.
62 F. V. Filson, *Matthew*, on Matthew 28:1–7.
63 E. Schweizer, *op.cit.*, on Mark 15:47.
64 W. Hendriksen, *John*, ad loc.
65 Quoted by Aquinas in *Catena Aurea*. cf C. E. B. Cranfield, *SJT* 5 (1952), p.194.
66 J. Calvin, *Harmony of Matthew, Mark and Luke* III, p.347.
67 Matthew 28:7; Mark 16:7; John 20:17.
68 It seems certain that the section from Mark 16:9–20 was not part of the original gospel, cf W. Lane, *op.cit.*, pp.501–505 for details of the evidence. However, the section was circulating around the middle of the second century and was probably written in the first half of the second century. It seems unlikely that verse 14, which is derogatory to the apostles would have been included at this stage if its basis in fact was not very strongly substantiated in the traditions of the early church. The existence of the Freer Logion, found after v.14 in the 4th century manuscript W, and making a defence for the apostles, strengthens this view, c.f. E. Schweizer, *Mark*, p.375, S. Johnson, *op.cit.*, p.266.
69 H. Anderson, *Mark*, on Mark 15:40–41.
70 C. F. D. Moule, *The Phenomenon of the New Testament*, pp.64–65.
71 cf L. Morris, *John*, commenting on John 4:27.
72 C. G. Montefiore, *The Synoptic Gospels* I, p.377.
73 cf R. Brown, 'Roles of Women in the Fourth Gospel', *Th.St.* 36 (1975), p.699.
74 cf p.50 above.
75 H. Küng, *On Being a Christian*, p.459.
76 *idem*.
77 The reference in Galatians 4:4 to Jesus being 'born of a woman' only reinforces the humanity of Jesus and is not significant for a study of Mary. We would follow G. B. Caird, *Revelation*, p.149, and G. R. Beasley-Murray, *Revelation*, p.189, in not accepting the view that sees the woman clothed with the sun in Revelation 12 as a description of Mary. This view is described fully by J. McHugh, *The Mother of Jesus in the New Testament*, pp.404–432.
78 A. George, 'Mary' in X. Léon-Dufour ed. *Dictionary of Biblical Theology*, pp.338–342.
79 J. McHugh, *op.cit.*, p.153.
80 C. Ryder Smith, *The Bible Doctrine of Womanhood*, p.119.
81 J. de Satgé (*Mary and the Christian Gospel*) in a slightly different form of this argument, accepts without question the supposition of Freud that to bring up a perfect child requires a perfect mother, describing perfection for Mary as 'so necessary to the awesome demands of her particular motherhood'. p.73.
82 K. Rahner, *Theological Investigations* I, p.209, cf pp.203–225.
83 J. McHugh, *op.cit.*, pp.51–52.
84 *idem*, p.403.
85 e.g. M. C. Shea, 'Cana', *The Downside Review* 95 (1977), pp.124–132.
86 cf R. Brown, 'Roles of Women in the Fourth Gospel', *Th.St.* 36 (1975), p.697.
87 J. McHugh, *op.cit.*, p.402.

CHAPTER FOUR

(pages 61 – 121)

1 E. Schweizer, *Church Order in the New Testament*, p.13.
2 Of the epistles attributed to Paul, there are particular difficulties in accepting Ephesians and the Pastoral Epistles as authentic. As far as Ephesians is concerned, C. L. Mitton *(Ephesians)* assesses the factors involved and concludes that 'the difficulties presented by an assumption of the direct Pauline authorship of Ephesians appear insuperable' (p.11 cf pp.2–11). However, we would dispute this and rather conclude with M. Barth *(Ephesians 1–3*, p.36f.) that 'in view of the insufficient linguistic and historical arguments and of the prejudicial character of the theological reasons exhibited against Ephesians it is advisable for the time being to consider Paul its author.' The discussion of Pauline authorship of the Pastorals is complicated by the fact that a major argument used is the contrast seen between the attitude to women found in the Pastorals and that found elsewhere in the Pauline corpus. We have concluded that this contrast is more apparent than real and for this reason among others we have followed J. N. D. Kelly *(The Pastoral Epistles)* and D. Guthrie *(The Pastoral Epistles)* in accepting Pauline authorship. Thus we will consider passages from both Ephesians and the Pastorals in the context of the teaching of Paul. However, as our primary concern is with the New Testament material as a whole rather than with developing a Pauline theology as such, it is important for our purposes that we investigate the teaching of these books, even if it were concluded that they were not written directly by Paul.
3 W. G. Kümmel, *Man in the New Testament*, p.83.
4 D. Cupitt, *Crisis of Moral Authority*, p.61. Until fairly recently for example, the influence of Aristotle's dualistic view of the world has been very strong. This view sees the world in terms of opposing forces and ideas, e.g. active, strong, stable, good, male as opposed to passive, weak, fickle, evil, female. It was this kind of thinking that gave credence to the view that women were to be avoided as the cause of evil desires and led to the idealization of celibacy.
5 e.g. W. D. Stacey, *The Pauline View of Man*; M. W. Robinson, *The Christian Doctrine of Man*; R. Bultmann, *Theology of the New Testament*; H. Conzelmann, *An Outline of the New Testament*; C. Ryder Smith, *The Bible Doctrine of Man*.
6 C. A. Anderson Scott, *Christianity According to Paul*.
7 E. Zabolai-Caekme, 'A Woman Looks at Theology', *Ecum.Rev.* 27 (1975), p.325.
8 C. F. H. Henry, 'Reflections on Women's Lib', *Ch.Tod.* 19 (1975), p.345.
9 L. Scanzoni & N. Hardesty, *All We're Meant to Be;* J. Harper, *Women and the Gospel*.
10 R. T. Beckwith & G. E. Duffield, 'Towards a Better Solution', *Ch.* 86 (1972), pp.110–112.
11 'There is no' rather than 'neither...nor...'.
12 G. B. Caird, 'Paul and Women's Liberty', *BJRL* 34 (1972), p.273.
13 *idem.*
14 R. Banks, 'Paul and Women's Liberation', *Interchange* 18 (1976), p.83.
15 M. C. Tenney, *Galatians*, p.129.
16 Romans 12:4–13; 13:8; 15:5; 1 Corinthians 12:25; Galatians 5:13; Ephesians 2:2,12,25,32; 5:21; 1 Thessalonians 3:12 etc..
17 C. R. Smith, *The Bible Doctrine of Womanhood*, p.81.
18 F. Fisher, *1 & 2 Corinthians*, p.173.

19 F. W. Grosheide, *1 Corinthians*, p.250.
20 G. E. Ladd, *A Theology of the New Testament*, p.328.
21 cf M. Barth, *Ephesians 4–6*, p.618.
22 S. Bedale, 'The Meaning of *Kephale* in Pauline Epistles', *JTS* 5 (1954), p.211.
23 cf pp.90–92 below, for a full discussion of this point.
24 E. Kähler (*Die Frau in den Paulinischen Briefen*, p.40) accepts that ruling is not the emphasis here but feels that to see headship as referring to 'source' raises problems in the God/Christ analogy leading to the implication that 'there was when Christ was not'. However, it seems unnecessary to press the analogy that far. H. Conzelmann (*1 Corinthians*) makes the point that 'Paul does not draw the conclusion of extending the relationship between God and Christ to become a real analogy of the relationship between Christ and man. Thus we have to exercise caution. Paul is concerned here with the headship of man and not with every other related question,' pp.183–184.
25 J. Chrysostom, *Homilies on the Epistle to the Corinthians*, p.150–151.
26 *idem* , E. Kähler *op.cit.*, p.40, also sees the real point of headship in this verse as unity. cf L. Scanzoni & N. Hardesty (*All We're Meant To Be*, p.22) who paraphrase this verse as, 'As Christ is one with God in substance, so the husband is one in flesh with his wife. Every Christian is united with Christ.' Also of R. Banks, 'Paul and Women's Liberation', *Interchange* 18 (1976), p.82.
27 cf p.71 below.
28 If so, then this could influence our view of what Paul was implying in 1 Corinthians 11, although of course he could be using the same metaphor in a slightly different way. In another context he does just this where the emphasis in his description of Christ as head over all (Ephesians 1:21–22) is completely different from that in his description of Christ as head of the church (Ephesians 4:15–16). In each of these occasions the 'head' is being used in a special sense, though it may be significant that in 1 Corinthians 12:21 the head is presented merely as one member among many.
29 cf p.75 below for a more complete discussion of this point.
30 G. Delling, *TDNT* VIII, pp.27–48.
31 Peter does use the terms together in 1 Peter 3:5–6, possibly indicating some relationship, but even there, they are not necessarily being used synonymously.
32 M. Barth, *op.cit.*, p.709.   33 *idem*, pp.710–711.
34 K. Barth, *Church Dogmatics*, III 4, p.172.
35 cf the discussion on pages 61–62 above.
36 G. B. Caird, 'Paul and Women's Liberty', *BJRL* 34 (1972), p.274.
37 *idem*, p.275. D. R. Cartlidge, '1 Corinthians 7 as a Foundation for a Christian Sex Ethic', *J. of R.* 55 (1975), p.220.
38 M. Lietzmann, *An die Korinther*, p.29.
39 D. S. Bailey, *The Man-Woman Relation in Christian Thought*, p.11.
40 D. R. Cartlidge, *op.cit.*, p.226.
41 R. Banks, 'Paul and Women's Liberation', *Interchange* 18 (1976), p.88.
42 H. Conzelmann, *1 Corinthians*, thinks it expresses Paul's own sentiments; but D. Cartlidge, *op.cit.*, P. Scroggs, 'Paul and the Eschatological Woman' *JAAR* 40 (1972), C. K. Barrett, 1 Corinthians, and F. F. Bruce, *1 and 2 Corinthians*, all see it as a quotation which Paul uses to make his point by limiting its application.
43 cf the discussion of 1 Corinthians 11:10, pp.90–92 below, and of 1 Timothy 2:12, pp.102–103 below.
44 R. Banks, *op.cit.*, p.85.
45 As it is not directly relevant to the area of male-female relationships, we have

not included here a discussion of the difficulties involved in the interpretation of verse 14, 'Otherwise your children would be unclean, but as it is they are holy'. Treatment of this issue can be found in C. K. Barrett, *1 Corinthians*, pp.164–166 or H. Conzelmann, *op.cit.*, pp.121–123.

46 J. K. Eliot, 'Paul's Teaching on Marriage in 1 Corinthians', *NTS* 19 (1972-3), p.219.
47 F. F. Bruce, *op.cit.*, pp.75–76.
48 J. Hering, *1 Corinthians*, p.61.
49 H. Conzelmann, *op.cit.*, p.134.
50 L. Morris, *1 Corinthians*, p.119.
51 E. Kahler, *Die Frau in den Paulinischen Briefen*, p.63.
52 While it is clear that there is a connection between verse 21 and the preceding section, nevertheless the omission of the verb from verse 22 means that it is strongly linked with verse 21, indicating that verse 21 is to be seen as an integral part of this section. This view is taken by F. F. Bruce, *Ephesians*, M. Barth, *Ephesians 4–6*, and T. K. Abbott, *Ephesians and Colossians*, although W. Hendriksen, *Ephesians*, and H. Conzelmann, *Die Kleineren Briefe des Apostels Paulus*, would disagree.
53 cf E. Kahler, *Die Frau in den Paulinischen Briefen*, pp.123–126.
54 M. Barth, *op.cit.*, p.655.
55 For example, G. B. Caird, *Principalities and Powers*, p.17ff, thinks that he is.
56 F. F. Bruce, *op.cit.*, p.114.
57 cf pp.67–68 above.
58 F. F. Bruce, *op.cit.*, p.114.
59 M. Barth, *op.cit.*, p.614,618.
60 E. Kähler, *op.cit.*, p.124.
61 J. Hurley, *Man and Woman in Biblical Perspective*, p.145.
62 F. F. Bruce, *op.cit.*, p.118.
63 G. B. Caird, *op.cit.*, p.21.
64 M. Barth, *op.cit.*, p.620.
65 C. L. Mitton, *Ephesians*, ad loc.
66 E. Kähler, *op.cit.*, p.125.
67 M. Barth, *op.cit.*, p.650.
68 W. Hendriksen, *Colossians and Philemon*, p.167; R. P. Martin, *Colossians and Philemon*, p.119.
69 cf pp.67–68 above.
70 R. P. Martin, *op.cit.*, p.119.
71 E. Lohse, *Colossians and Philemon*, p.158.
72 F. F. Bruce in E. K. Simpson and F. F. Bruce, *Ephesians and Colossians*, p.287.
73 C. F. D. Moule, *Colossians and Philemon*, p.127. cf pp.73–74 above.
74 K. Stendahl, *The Bible and the Role of Women*, p.31.
75 D. Guthrie, *The Pastoral Epistles*, p.104.
76 C. K. Barrett, *The Pastoral Epistles*, p.71.
77 M. Dibelius and H. Conzelmann, *The Pastoral Epistles*, p.75.
78 J. N. D. Kelly, *The Pastoral Epistles*, p.115.
79 K. H. Rengstorf, *TDNT* II, p.49.
80 R. A. Ward, *1 and 2 Timothy and Titus*, p.86.
81 A. R. C. Leaney, *Timothy, Titus and Philemon*, p.120.
82 M. Barth, *op.cit.*, p.712.
83 O. A. Piper, *The Christian Interpretation of Sex*, p.158.
84 In speaking of the relationship of women to the church, it should be noted that we are not primarily concerned with the relation of women to men within the church community, but rather with her relation to the whole

community consisting of both men and women.

85 C. F. D. Moule, *Worship in the New Testament*, p.6ɔ
86 *idem.*
87 G. B. Caird, 'Paul and Women's Liberty', *BJRL* 54 (1972), p.278.
88 W. O. Walker in '1 Corinthians 11:2–16 and Paul's Views regarding Women' *JBL* 94 (1975), p.94, comes to the conclusion that this passage is a non-Pauline interpolation consisting of three separate pericopae; but there is no manuscript evidence for this, and the majority of scholars have no doubts at all about its Pauline origin.
89 E. Kähler, *Die Frau in den Paulinischen Briefen*, p.34.
90 e.g. F. F. Bruce, *1 & 2 Corinthians*, H. Conzelmann, *1 Corinthians*, C. K. Barrett, *1 Corinthians*, F. Fisher, *1 & 2 Corinthians*, J. Héring, *1 Corinthians*, etc.
91 As does J. Hurd, *The Origin of 1 Corinthians*, pp.182–184.
92 cf J. B. Hurley, *Man and Woman in 1 Corinthians*, p.41–42; C. K. Barrett, *op.cit.*, p.247; F. F. Bruce, *op.cit.*, p.103.
93 As does W. J. Martin in '1 Corinthians 11:2–16: An Interpretation' in W. Gasque and R. P. Martin edit. *Apostolic History and the Gospel*, p.231.
94 Fisher and Hodge take this view though Barrett and Grosheide dispute it. It remains unclear why the term 'every male' is used but as this is not the main point at issue, it may just be a matter of literary convenience. We cannot draw the conclusion from this that Christ is head of the male, even the Christian male, in a way that excludes his headship of the female. Conzelmann's warning (cf p.153 note 24 above) must be kept in mind here.
95 Bruce, Conzelmann et al. take the former view; Fisher, Grosheide, Hering et al. the latter.
96 J. B. Hurley, *op.cit.*, cf his article 'Did Paul Require Veils?' *W.Th.J.* 35 (1972), pp.190–192.
97 G. W. Knight, *The New Testament Teaching on the Role Relationship of Male and Female.*
98 D. S. Bailey, *The Man-Woman Relation in Christian Thought*, p.15.
99 M. Goguel, *The Primitive Church*, p.549.
100 F. F. Bruce, *op.cit.*, p.103.
101 J. Chrysostom, *Homilies on the Epistles to the Corinthians*, p.150. cf K. Barth, *Church Dogmatics III 4*, p.173 for further discussion on this argument.
102 F. F. Bruce, *op.cit.*, p.104; cf C. K. Barrett, *op.cit.*, p.250; Chrysostom, *op.cit.*, p.150; Caird, *op.cit.*, p.271, etc.
103 N. Weeks, 'Of Silence and Head Covering', *W.Th.f.* 35 (1972), pp.21–27.
104 To use 'for' or 'as' here rather than 'instead of' as we are forced to do if we assume that the custom Paul is dealing with is the wearing of a covering (cf AV, RSV, ASV), is to make a deliberate change in the normal usage of the Greek word *anti.*
105 J. Hurley, 'Did Paul Require Veils?', *W.Th.J.* 35 (1972), pp.190–220.
106 cf Leviticus 16 where the high priest is told to wear a turban, etc.
107 S. A. Reynolds, *W.Th.J.* 36 (1973), pp.90–91; W. J. Martin, '1 Corinthians 11:2–16 : An Interpretation', pp.231–241.
108 W. J. Martin, *op.cit.*, p.239.
109 C. K. Barrett, *1 Corinthians*, p.250.
110 F. F. Bruce, *1 & 2 Corinthians*, p.104.
111 M. Hooker, 'Authority on her Head', *NTS* 10 (1963–4), p.410.
112 N. Weeks, *op.cit.*, p.21ff.
113 C. K. Barrett, *op.cit.*, p.251.
114 G. W. Knight, 'Male and Female Related He Them', *Ch.Tod.* 21 ₁ɜ/5), p.710.

115 F. Fisher, *op.cit.*, p.176.
116 cf pp.14–17 above.
117 G. B. Caird, *Principalities and Powers*, pp.17–22. cf T. C. Craig, *The Interpreters Bible*, Vol. 10, p.127.
118 K. Stendahl, *The Bible and the Role of Women*, p.29; H. Conzelmann, p.136; F. Fisher, p.176.
119 A. Feuillet, 'L'homme gloire de Dieu et la femme gloire de l'homme'; *Rev.Bib.* 81 (1974), p.180, 'elle est, a l'égal de l'homme, une image de Dieu et elle est en même temps la gloire et la fierté de l'homme.'
120 C. Hodge, *1 Corinthians*, F. Fisher, *op.cit.*
121 For a full discussion of this point see M. Hooker, *art.cit.*, also J. Hurley, *art.cit.*, pp.206–212, and C. K. Barrett, *op.cit.*, p.254.
122 G. Kittel, *TDNT* II '*exousia*'.
123 R. Banks, 'Paul and Women's Liberation', *Interchange* 18 (1976), p.93.
124 J. A. Fitzmeyer, 'A Feature of Qumran Angelology and the Angels of 1 Corinthians 11:10', *NTS* 4 (1957/8), pp.48–58, where the different views are clearly set out.
125 G. B. Caird, 'Paul and Women's Liberty', *BJRL* 34 (1972), p.278.
126 cf F. F. Bruce, *op.cit.*, p.106.
127 cf M. Hooker, *art.cit.*, though it is hard to see how a covering hides one from God, especially if the covering is merely long hair or hair worn in a particular style.
128 J. Héring, *1 Corinthians*, p.108.
129 This approach involves seeing the covering in the earlier verses as a symbol of submission and in verse 10 as a symbol of authority. This would appear to raise certain difficulties, although Hurley does not seem to find it a problem.
130 D. S. Bailey, *op.cit.*, p.283.
131 cf note 104, p.155 above.
132 C. K. Barrett, *op.cit.*, p.257.
133 G. B. Caird, *art.cit.*, p.270.
134 F. Fisher, *op.cit.*, p.179.
135 J. C. Greig, 'Women's Hats – 1 Corinthians 11:1–16', *Exp.T.* 69 (1958), p.156.
136 F. F. Bruce, *op.cit.*, p.108; C. K. Barrett, *op.cit.*, p.259.
137 E. Kähler, *op.cit.*, cf H. Conzelmann, *op.cit.*, p.191.
138 H. Conzelmann, *op.cit.*, p.182, thinks that the chapter has the appearance of this kind of discussion.
139 There is a divergence of opinions as to whether the section begins with verse 34 or with verse 33b. We have assumed the former here for two reasons, firstly because of the clumsy nature of a single sentence containing the two phrases 'in all the churches' and 'in the churches', and secondly because in the documents where textual transposition does occur, verses 34 and 35 are always linked together without verse 33b.
140 H. Conzelmann, *1 Corinthians*, p.246. cf. A. Oekpe, '*gunē*' *TDNT* Vol.1.
141 Headed by D.G.88.
142 C. K. Barrett, *1 Corinthians*, p.332.
143 F. W. Grosheide, *1 Corinthians*, p.342. cf. G. Ladd, *A Theology of the New Testament*, p.528.
144 P. K. Jewett, *Man as Male and Female*, p.115. H. Conzelmann, *op.cit.*, p.246 also points out the contradictions can only be resolved by the construction of some hypothetical scheme or arbitrary limitation.
145 A. Robertson and A. Plummer, *1 Corinthians*, p.324.
146 L. Birney, *The Role of Women in the New Testament Church*, p.15.
147 F. Fisher, *1 & 2 Corinthians*, p.231; J. Héring, *1 Corinthians*, p.154; M.

Henry, *Commentary*, p.583.
148 R. P. Martin, *1 Corinthians – Galatians*, p.45.
149 R. Banks, 'Paul and Women's Liberation', *Interchange* 18 (1976), p.94.
150 K. Stendahl, *The Bible and the Role of Women*, p.30.
151 F. F. Bruce, *1 & 2 Corinthians*, p.135.
152 L. Birney, *op.cit.*, p.15. cf G. W. Knight, *The New Testament Teaching on the Role and Relationships of Males and Females*.
153 cf pages 11–21 above.
154 J. B. Hurley, 'Did Paul Require Veils or the Silence of Women?' *W.Th.J.* 35 (1972), pp.190–220.
155 E. Kähler, *Die Frau in den Paulinischen Briefen*, p.61.
156 C. K. Barrett, *op.cit.*, p.330.
157 cf pp.51–53 above.
158 J. A. Anderson, *Woman's Warfare and Ministry*, pp.20–25. cf J. Harper, *Women and the Gospel*, p.8ff.
159 S. Aalen, 'A Rabbinic Formula in 1 Corinthians 14:34; *St.Ev.* II, p.513–525.
160 J. Calvin, *Corinthians* I, p.474.
161 cf note 2, p.152 above.
162 B. W. Powers, 'Women in the Church: The Application of 1 Timothy 2:8–15' *Interchange* 17 (1975), p.58.
163 cf D. J. Moo, 1 Timothy 2:11–15, Meaning – Significance, *Trinity Journal* 1 (1980), p.63.
164 W. Hendriksen, *1 & 2 Timothy and Titus*; J. N. D. Kelly, *The Pastoral Epistles*; C. K. Barrett, *The Pastoral Epistles*; R. Banks, 'Paul and Women's Liberation', *Interchange*, 18 (1976), pp.81–105.
165 M. Dibelius and H. Conzelmann, *The Pastoral Epistles*; D. Guthrie, *The Pastoral Epistles*; L. Birney, *The Role of Women in the New Testament Church*.
166 A. D. B. Spencer, 'Eve at Ephesus', *JETS* 17 (1974), pp.216–218.
167 G. Abbott-Smith, *A Manual Greek Lexicon of the New Testament*, p.277.
168 M. Dibelius & H. Conzelmann, *op.cit.*, p.47.
169 R. A. Ward, *1 & 2 Timothy and Titus*, p.51.
170 A. D. B. Spencer, *art.cit.*, p.218.
171 *idem* , p.218.
172 Any contradiction then arising between this passage and other Pauline teaching have been used by several scholars as a major argument for disputing the Pauline origin of the epistle. cf note 2, p.152 above.
173 D. Guthrie, *op.cit.*, p.76.
174 B. W. Powers, *op.cit.*, p.57.
175 D. J. Moo (art.cit., pp.65–68) prefers to see the teaching and the having authority as 'two distinct yet related activities'. He would suggest that teaching by its nature involves authority, therefore the use of the additional term must imply a separate additional prohibition. He argues that the use of *oude*, 'nor', supports this view.
176 cf p.71 above.   177 T. Magister, 18:8.
178 N. J. Hommes, 'Let Women be Silent in Church', *Calv.Th.J.* 4 (1969), p.19.
179 M. Dibelius and H. Conzelmann, *op.cit.*, p.47.
180 J. A. Anderson, *Woman's Warfare and Ministry*, p.30.
181 J. N. D. Kelly, *op.cit.*, p.68.
182 D. Guthrie, *op.cit.*, p.77.
183 G. W. Knight, *The New Testament Teaching on the Role Relationship of Male and Female*, p.5.
184 pp.14–17 above.
185 J. Calvin, *Pastoral Epistles*, p.70.

186 A. Stibbs in *New Bible Commentary Revised* (ed. D. Guthrie & A. Motyer), p.1171.
187 B. S. Easton, *The Pastoral Epistles*, p.124. cf J. N. D. Kelly, *op.cit.*, p.68; D. Guthrie, *op.cit.*, p.77; R. A. Ward, *op.cit.*, p.52; K. Stendahl, *The Bible and the Role of Women*, p.28.
188 cf D. Cupitt, *Crisis in Moral Authority*, p.67.
189 W. Hendriksen, *op.cit.*, p.109.
190 A. T. Hanson (*Studies in the Pastoral Epistles*, pp.65–77) concludes that in the Pastorals, unlike other Pauline writing, Eve's sin is assumed to be sexual in character. However if this were so, it is difficult to see why this should be used in an argument restricting the teaching of women.
191 N. J. Hommes, *op.cit.*, p.10.
192 A. D. B. Spencer, *op.cit.*, pp.220–221.
193 cf pp.126–130 below.
194 e.g. Colossians 1:28; 3:16; Romans 15:14; 1 Corinthians 1:5; 14:26; Ephesians 5:19. Also in 2 Timothy 2:2 Timothy is exhorted to entrust his message to faithful men who will be able to teach others also. The word used here for men is not *anēr*, which would refer specifically to males, but *anthrōpos*, which refers to mankind in a much more general sense (like the German word *Mensch*) and which, although it could be being used in a restricted sense, could also have been specifically chosen to include women as well as men.
195 C. K. Barrett, *op.cit.*, p.56.
196 D. Guthrie, *op.cit.*, pp.77–78.
197 cf A. R. C. Leaney, *Timothy, Titus and Philemon*, p.54.
198 N. J. Hommes, *op.cit.*, p.21.
199 R. A. Ward, *op.cit.*, p.53.
200 G. W. Knight, *The New Testament Teaching on the Role Relationship of Male and Female*, p.9.
201 Romans 15:14; Colossians 3:16; 1 Timothy 5:17, etc.
202 N. J. Hommes, 'Let Women be Silent in Church', *Calv.Th.J.* 4 (1969), p.15.
203 pp.123–126 below.
204 W. Schmithals, *The Office of Apostle in the Early Church*, p.21.
205 e.g. 1 Corinthians 16:16; 1 Thessalonians 5:12.
206 J. Daniélou, *The Ministry of Women in the Early Church*, p.10.
207 E. Schweizer, *Church Order in the New Testament*, p.229.
208 Romans 16:7; Galatians 1:19; 1 Corinthians 9:6. W. Schmithals (*op.cit.*, pp.67—95) would in fact dispute that Paul classified all the Twelve as apostles. cf pp.49–51 above.
209 M. Dibelius and H. Conzelmann, *The Pastoral Epistles*, pp.55–57; C. K. Barrett, *The Pastoral Epistles*, pp.57–58.
210 The word *presbuteros* (plural *presbuteroi*) basically just means 'older man', hence 'elder'.
211 A. E. Harvey, 'Elders', *JTS* 25 (1974), p.326.
212 A possible argument against this is found in 1 Timothy 5, where in verse 1 Timothy is told, 'do not rebuke an older man', that is, a *presbuteros*. The older versions translate this as 'elder', presumably supported by verse 17, 'let the elders (*presbuteroi*) who rule well be considered worthy of double honour'. If this is correct, it would be logical to translate the feminine *presbuteras* of verse 2, 'treat older women like mothers', as 'elders', also, particularly as if the writer had wanted to avoid any parallel with the men he would have chosen the alternative word for older women, *presbutidas* (Titus 2:3).
213 J. N. D. Kelly, *The Pastoral Epistles*; C. K. Barrett, *op.cit.*; R. A. Ward, *1 & 2 Timothy and Titus*, and W. Hendriksen, *1 & 2 Timothy and Titus*, take the

former view; B. S. Easton, *The Pastoral Epistles* and A. R. C. Leaney, *Timothy, Titus and Philemon*, the latter.
214 cf Phoebe, Romans 16:1, also the reference in Pliny *Letters* X 96, to certain women who were called deacons (*ancillae quae ministrae dicebantur*).
215 J. N. D. Kelly, *op.cit.*, p.112.
216 R. McGlashan, 'Diakonia and the Diaconate', *Churchman* 84 (1970), pp.128–9.
217 R. Banks, 'Paul and Women's Liberation', *Interchange* 18 (1976), p.104.
218 e.g. G. W. Knight, *The New Testament Teaching on the Role Relationship of Male and Female*, pp.6–7; G. G. Blum, 'The Office of Women in the New Testament', *Churchman* 85 (1971), pp.175–189; F. Fisher, *1 & 2 Corinthians*, p.175ff.
219 pp.11–22 above.
220 pp.65–69 above.
221 D. S. Bailey, *The Man-Woman Relation in Christian Thought*, p.301.
222 *idem.*
223 e.g. Romans 13:1ff; 1 Corinthians 14:23; 1 Timothy 3:7; Titus 2:5,8,10; 3:11.
224 A. M. Stibbs, *1 Peter*, p.123. cf 1 Peter 2:15,20; 3:4.
225 E. G. Selwyn, *1 Peter*, p.183. cf 1 Peter 2:12,15; 3:1–2,16.
226 As suggested by F. W. Beare, 1 Peter, p.131; C. Spicq, *Les Epîtres de Saint Pierre*, p.115; J. N. D. Kelly, *The Epistles of Peter and Jude*, p.127.
227 cf E. Best, *1 Peter*, p.124.
228 E. G. Selwyn, *op.cit.*, p.182.
229 cf F. W. Beare, *op.cit.*, p.127. cf H. C. Kee & F. W. Young, *The Living World of the New Testament*, p.442.
230 C. Spicq, *op.cit.*, p.118.
231 A. M. Stibbs, *op.cit.*, p.124.
232 E. G. Selwyn, *op.cit.*, p.183.
233 cf E. Best, *op.cit.*, pp.126–127.
234 J. Chrysostom, *Homilies on the Epistles to the Corinthians*, p.155.
235 E. Selwyn, *op.cit.*, p.186, following Bengel, *Gnomon of the N.T.* ad loc.
236 F. W. Beare, *op.cit.*, p.132.
237 A. M. Stibbs, *op.cit.*, p.127.
238 K. Stendahl, *The Bible and the Role of Women*, p.31.
239 C. Spicq, *op.cit.*, p.124.
240 E. Best, *op.cit.*, p.128.

CHAPTER FIVE

(pages 122 – 130)

1 cf p.124 below.
2 Acts 18:2–3,18,26; Romans 16:3; 1 Corinthians 16:19; 2 Timothy 4:19.
3 The editors of some copies of the text of Acts reversed the order in Acts 18:26 placing Aquila before Priscilla. That they bothered to do so indicates that they at least did see the order as being of some significance. For the tendency of the Western text to lessen the importance of women, see E. Haenchen, *Acts*, p.508; F. F. Bruce, *Acts*, p.352; C. S. C. Williams, *Acts*, p.199.
4 cf W. Neil, *Acts*, p.194; E. Haenchen, *Acts*, p.550.
5 pp.108–113 above.
6 C. K. Barrett, *Romans*, p.283. cf M. Black, *Romans;* F. F. Bruce, *Romans;* A. M. Hunter, *Romans;* E. Brunner, *Romans*, ad loc.

7 J. Murray, *Romans*, p.229.
8 F. F. Bruce, op.cit., p.271. cf L. Scanzoni & N. Hardesty, *All We're Meant To Be*, p.63.
9 M. Goguel, *The Primitive Church*, p.553.
10 *The Homilies of St John Chrysostom*, Vol.11, p.555. It is interesting that in spite of Chrysostom's clear statement, the editors of the English translation of his works felt bound to add a footnote pointing out that Chrysostom must have been wrong on one of the two points for 'it is out of the question' for a woman to have been an apostle!
11 J. Foster, 'St Paul and Women', *Ext.T.* 62 (1951), p.376.
12 3 John has certain personal references which point strongly to it being written to an individual Christian but also certain exhortations which look very much as if they are addressed to a church community. Scholars are therefore divided in their opinion as to whether the 'elect lady' was an individual or a church. If she was in fact the leader of a church, the problem is solved. c.f. E. Timiadis 'From the Margin to the Forefront', *Ecum.Rev.* 27 1975, p.373.
13 J. Murray, *op.cit.*, p.226.
14 cf pp.111–112 above.
15 F. J. Leenhardt, *Romans*, p.379. cf C. E. B. Cranfield, *Romans II*, p.781; M. Black, *Romans*, p.178; A. Nygren, *Romans*, p.456.
16 cf M. Black, *op.cit.*, p.179; A. M. Hunter, *op.cit.*, p.130.
17 G. C. Blum, 'The Office of Women in the New Testament', *Churchman* 85 (1971), p.175.
18 F. J. Leenhardt, *op.cit.*, p.379.
19 R. Banks, 'Paul and Women's Liberation', *Interchange* 18 (1976), p.90.
20 E. Ellis, 'Paul and his Co-Workers', *NTS* 17 (1971), p.437.
21 E. Haenchen, *Acts*, p.154.
22 Including Matthias.
23 We follow Barrett, Black, Cranfield etc. in accepting chapter 16 as an integral part of Romans.
24 cf p.124 above.
25 M. Goguel, *The Primitive Church*, p.552.
26 J. Daniélou, *The Ministry of Women in the Early Church*, p.8.
27 W. D. Thomas, 'The Place of Women in the Church at Philippi', *Exp.T.* 83 (1972), p.117.
28 *idem*, p.118.
29 G. G. Blum, 'The Office of Women in the New Testament', *Ch.* 85 (1971), p.175.
30 M. Goguel, *op.cit.*, p.552.
31 W. D. Thomas, *art.cit.*, p.119.
32 *idem*.
33 G. G. Blum, *op.cit.*, p.175.
34 R. Banks, 'Paul and Women's Liberation', *Interchange* 18 (1976), p.90.